MW01029736

Also by
Chad Sanders

Black Magic: What Black Leaders Learned from Trauma and Triumph

HOW TO SELL OUT

The (Hidden) Cost of Being a Black Writer

—— ◆ ◆ ◆ ◆ ◆ ——

CHAD SANDERS

SIMON & SCHUSTER
New York Amsterdam/Antwerp London
Toronto Sydney New Delhi

Simon & Schuster
1230 Avenue of the Americas
New York, NY 10020

First Simon & Schuster hardcover edition February 2025

Some names and identifying characteristics have been changed. The characters and events depicted in Chapter 4, "*The Tournament*: 'Pilot,'" are fictitious and all the names and events in the pilot are the products of the author's imagination.

Interior design by Lewelin Polanco

Manufactured in the United States of America

1 3 5 7 9 10 8 6 4 2

Library of Congress Cataloging-in-Publication Data is available.

ISBN 978-1-9821-9083-5
ISBN 978-1-9821-9087-3 (ebook)

Contents

HOW TO SELL OUT

1

The First Hit Changes You

This is my last time writing about race.

Just a few years ago I would have done nearly anything for a chance to make a living as a working creative. I know that because I did things I once thought were beneath me for a shot at that life. This life. I contorted my personality and told myself lies to maintain friendships with people who had access and relationships that could help me find opportunities to write for notable publications and networks. I wrote full feature films and TV pilots for free for tasteless producers, hoping to get into their good graces and find my way through *their* networks to the people I actually wanted to work with. I lived without income for months at a time. I broke up with other friends—*real friends*—because I couldn't afford to attend their weddings and birthday celebrations but didn't have the stomach to tell them. I needed the money. I needed it to stay afloat while I hustled to get TV writing jobs and to get my first book published.

It became easy to lie to others about my choices; I had plenty of practice from lying to myself. I told myself a story: that each step I took further into the Hollywood labyrinth was a necessary choice, an *authentic* choice, to keep my dream of becoming a professional writer alive. As a striving professional storyteller, it was easy to tell myself a story. And it was vital. I was working toward a pipe dream, and the most important person I needed to sell on my potential to achieve that dream was me. The lies needed to be taut, impenetrable, *believable.*

I wasn't a broke, lonely, starving artist wannabe isolating himself and ruining his job prospects by holing up in coffee shops every day to use the free Wi-Fi while clicking at my screenplays—*I was an inspired go-getter with unrealized potential sacrificing for his dream.* I wasn't scared, *I was exhilarated.* I wasn't crazy, *I was a risk-taker.* I wasn't tripping, *I was unconventional.*

These weren't my first doses of self-delusion. I'd taken my first hits years ago, swallowing down bucketfuls of insidious lies well before I left corporate America to try my hand as a writer. I let myself believe in the extended hand of white allyship. I let myself believe that over the past decade some piece of our country had taken an earnest account of its repeated atrocities against Black people, and that by way of repair, Black voices like mine would now be rewarded for speaking up.

Those miscalculations led me to the most absurd and ridiculous lie among them, but it was one that I truly believed: I thought that I could sell away my Black perspective, my experiences, my hardships, even my joys, and that the cost of doing so would be something that I could bear. I thought trading my voice for money and fame would make for a good deal, a deal I could sustain, a deal I could *win.* And I came to that ridiculous conclusion, that self-exposure and a bit of self-betrayal are worth it for the right price, in the same place that

I learned that everything a person has—their identity, their image, their words, their opinions, their entire existence—must be for sale. I learned that in the tech industry.

In 2016 I worked at a small tech startup on Wall Street where we taught coding skills to people who wanted to leave their jobs to become software engineers. Our business had three locations—San Francisco, Chicago, and New York. I was the head of partnerships in the New York office. My job was to form relationships with other tech startups so that they would hire our students once they finished our nineteen-week coding boot camp. In order to form those relationships, I spent much of my time schmoozing white tech bros who were CEOs and VPs at the tech startups with whom we needed partnership. Almost all of the CEOs and VPs were men, and I'd meet them out in Manhattan several times each week for endless pints of IPAs, baseball games, electronic dance music shows, and other stuff white people like.

I was good at the job of schmoozing white guys because I had learned how to disarm them and make them comfortable at my previous employer—*Google*. It was there that I learned that as a Black person, my sole presence in a social environment made liberal, white, techy people feel a sense of self-satisfaction; my presence made them feel that they had *done the work* of diversifying their community. As long as I was there with them in the Penny Farthing bar on East Thirteenth Street, chugging down booze and over-laughing at their jokes and rapping along to 50 Cent with them, they weren't racist. How could they be? Look how cozy they were with this Black hipster.

But just sitting there and chumming it up with those early-thirties tech bros wasn't enough to get them to do business with me. No. They lived a life where most people around them bent to make them comfortable. Their skyscraping, modern apartment buildings came with Black and brown doormen who complimented their new Patagonia vests and Jordan sneakers as they left their buildings. Those same doormen had secret handshakes with them to make them look cool to the women they brought home from the douche bars in the East Village and Williamsburg late at night. And in return, those doormen got tipped and got to keep their jobs.

But I wasn't trying to be a doorman for these guys. I was trying to do business. Five-dollar tips weren't going to be enough. I needed $50K tips from them to help keep our startup alive. I needed these guys to see me as someone closer to eye level. I watched the way that these white guys pushed each other around in conversation as a way of holding the balance among them.

One weeknight I went to meet up with two co-CEOs of a tech startup that had raised over $40 million with no profitability. I learned later that one of the guys, the douchier one, was the son of one of the wealthiest corporate attorneys in the world. This company was basically a pet project for him, let's call him Owen. Owen had never led a successful business of any kind, but Daddy had helped him line up several major investors. Owen's partner, who we'll call Brett, had previously worked at a giant social media company. They were both about ten years older than me, in their mid-thirties. They were, of course, both white. Extra-white. Owen wore a button-up shirt and khakis everywhere, no matter what location or time of year. Brett was the sort of white guy who called every guy "brother."

I was first to arrive at the Hair of the Dog sports bar on the Lower East Side for our *meeting*. This was our fifth time getting together socially, and my mission was to finally close them on giving our startup some money in exchange for getting first dibs on employing our students after graduation. Closing the deal had proved slippery for me. Each time we got together, we drank a lot, we talked about their lives, and their interests, and Owen's obsession with Asian women (yikes), but whenever I tried to move the conversation over to business, they diverted. Brett would make a joke about me being a "hustla'—always on the grind," and they'd turn the conversation to another shot or comment on one of the games on TV.

I was always on time for our meetups, and they were always late. That's because my ambitions for these hangouts were very different from theirs. I wanted their money. They wanted a friend. I think underneath it all, that was very clear to all three of us. But they had the upper hand because I never set a boundary or told them that I needed to close this deal or walk away. More importantly, they were older than me, richer than me, and infinitely whiter than I was, no matter how many pints of IPA beer I drank.

I was also going through an identity transition at the time. With the freedom I'd taken by leaving Google, I was starting to figure out how I wanted to look. I had thrown away my own pale blue button-up shirts and khakis, which had served as my Silicon Valley uniform, and replaced them with a set of all-black Feathers brand T-shirts and black joggers. I was growing my hair into a Mohawk of skinny twists; it was the first time since I was two years old that I'd let my hair grow out, coarse and curly on the top of my head. But I still wore Sperry shoes and thick-framed Warby Parker glasses. I was trim and still looked like a teenager in the face. I was like Frankenstein's monster, transforming from what Silicon Valley had made me into myself.

So while I was starting to look the part of someone who had his own point of view, I still strongly deferred to the voices and wants of these two rich white boys who kept calling me back for more beers and more hockey games on TV. But this time was going to be different. The last time the three of us had gotten together, Owen pissed me off. Weeks prior, in another dreadful sports bar with music so loud it could make your eyes bleed, the three of us sat at the bar waiting for our drinks. Owen had just detailed to us a hookup he'd had with one of his employees, which he described as a feat because she was dating the CEO of a competing tech startup in Union Square. As he wrapped up his story, he described the employee as being half white and half Asian, "the perfect mix, you know?" Brett nodded along. I must not have given Owen enough of a reaction. He continued.

"You're not into that, Chad?" he spat at me. "Oh, I know what you like."

He gestured at the bartender, who was still within earshot, on the other side of the bar.

"Dat assssss."

Brett and Owen chortled. I was furious, for me and her, but I played it off. Because of the check dangling at the end of the fishing pole. I was still trying to make these guys like me enough to give me money so I could get a bonus and a raise and more money and continue to schmooze more people with money and continue the cycle.

But I went home that night and couldn't shake the anger. These two guys were always poking each other, play-fighting, making fun of each other's parents, even going as far as to say they were gonna do sex acts on each other's moms and sisters. And I knew my Blackness was apparent to them, especially when I heard them correct themselves when they'd call LeBron James "articulate" or used the term "ghetto" to describe a wobbly barstool. But neither of them had ever directly weaponized race against me or anyone else for a laugh in my presence.

I took the long-ass subway ride from Lower Manhattan to Harlem, stewing the entire time. When I got home, I sat on my couch in my little one-bedroom apartment on 119th and Frederick Douglass thinking about why I was so mad. I blamed myself for letting them feel too comfortable around me. I blamed myself for all the jokes at *other people's* expense I'd laughed at hoping to endear myself to these guys and get their money. I felt terrible for not checking in with the bartender to see if she'd overheard. I felt like such a coward. And I was so angry that Owen had poked me right in the nose that way. He must have known I was a coward. Or maybe he just got off on trying to find out.

I thought about what I could do. I still very much needed to close this deal. Our startup wasn't profitable, and the upside for my equity in the company depended on deals like this. And this one seemed as close to the goal line as any I was developing at that time. My heart wanted justice, revenge, comeuppance for Owen. I considered simply ghosting these two guys and lying to my bosses that the deal just fell through. I considered telling my bosses the truth—that Owen was a racist asshole and I didn't want to ever see him again, so we should either forfeit the deal or hand off the relationship to a white person. But my bosses were early-thirties white guys just like Owen, with their own habits that I interpreted as microaggressions and outright racism. I imagined that if I told them about what happened with me and Owen, they'd stop seeing me as cool, smart, effective Chad and start seeing me as dangerous, alarm-triggering, Black Chad. And that would probably get me fired in short order. Then, I'd *really* need some money.

So for weeks, I said nothing of that moment to Owen and Brett. I pretended to ignore what happened. Consciously, I didn't even realize how much I was holding on to it. But I was obsessed with that moment. I played it and replayed it over and over in my head. I imagined myself throwing an entire tray of limes onto Owen's face and button-up shirt right there at the bar. I peeled Owen's character apart in my head. I imagined how insecure he must be around Brett, who was naturally better looking, more charming, and *didn't* have a super wealthy, domineering asshole father funding his life. Meanwhile, I took note of things about Brett that I had overlooked: how he nudged the people around him when he made a joke to get them to laugh because he wasn't sure if he was funny. How he only knew how to communicate with women by talking down to them because he didn't want them looking him right in the eye. How popular slang always rolled off his tongue so awkwardly, as if he were testing it with me for the first time.

And then, as I explored my memories of Owen, I realized something important. Something I could leverage. He weaponized my Blackness in that one disgusting moment because he fetishized my Blackness. I thought of how he curled his face up to look cool each time he dapped me. I remembered the way he'd position his feet up on a chair or out in the aisle in restaurants to make sure I got a look at his sneakers, so that I'd comment and affirm that he'd bought the right ones. I took note of how he'd force his way into conversations Brett and I had about basketball and rap, even though he clearly wasn't a fan of either.

It occurred to me that all this time I was offering Owen something in exchange for money that he already had way too much of: deference. *Now*, as I obsessed over the way he dehumanized me, I realized I had something much more valuable to him that I had been hiding when I could have been leveraging it. He didn't want a friend. He wanted a *Black* friend. He wanted Blackness.

And I still wanted his money.

So, that night at Hair of the Dog, I sat eagerly waiting for Owen and Brett to show up. I was almost giddy. Because tonight things were going to go differently: I was going to offer Owen what he'd wanted all along. I was going to give him Blackness. I sat at a table in the corner with my legs spread and my hands behind my head swallowing down a Maker's Mark on the rocks. Brett showed up first and we made casual conversation, but I was barely there. I was fixated, waiting for Owen.

Owen walked in and shared a long, overdone embrace with the

giant Black bouncer at the door, making a show to the crowded bar of how comfortable he was with the only other Black person in there besides me and a handful of the staff. I tracked him as he walked to the bar, grabbed his drink, then snuck up behind Brett and *snatched* his hat off his head, asserting his dominance. Brett took the hat back and hugged him.

Owen made his way over to me and reached his hand out to dap me. I gave him the strongest, most aerodynamically sound dap possible and the loud pop reverberated across the bar.

"Jeez, dude," he joked, shaking the sting out of his hand.

He sat and we grazed on wings as Owen and Brett chattered. But I wasn't normal. I was waiting, like a patient praying mantis waiting to strike as soon as Owen gave me an in to let him know how I felt about him. Their conversation turned to an employee who was highly qualified but struggling at their company. They often overshared about their employees and what was going on at their company, and they told me they were doing so to give me a window into what my life would be like if I ever made it into the C-suite as they had. But it always felt like they were just taking up all the oxygen in our conversations. Usually, I just nodded along and said "Wow, that's crazy" or "No way, they really did that?"

But this time I wanted action. The employee in question was named Sydney, and I could tell she was Black by how they talked around her Blackness. In their description they mentioned that she was "really cool most of the time, but a little intense" and that I—specifically—would really love working with her. White people often tell me that I'll love getting to know or working with another Black person they know.

Brett mentioned that Sydney, who ranked highly in their sales division, was having a hard time finding her voice in meetings with company leadership and that she was often taking long breaks during the day to take calls in the hallways or outside the office. Who was she talking to? Why did she seem so distracted at work? And then Owen asked the most un-self-aware question imaginable.

"Why does she take all her calls outside? Like, does she not trust us?"

I felt heat run up my legs into my chest and head. It was adrenaline. I was about to break the rules of our social dynamic. My hands went cold, and I blurted:

"Of course she doesn't trust you."

I said it with a cheeky smile on my face, like I was telling someone a juicy secret I'd been holding on to for the first time.

Owen and Brett looked at me more intently than ever before. Their eyes told me to continue.

"I mean . . . she's Black, right?" I asked rhetorically. It was obvious that she was.

"Owen, you're the whitest person I know, and I know *a lot* of white people." Owen stared. Brett held back a creeping smile.

"What do you mean?" Owen said seriously. He was in shock and curious. I scrolled through the mental notes I'd taken on his character in the weeks since I'd last seen him.

"I mean, you talk to every Black person like they're your personal help staff. You dress like you're going to a city council meeting every day. You *literally* called LeBron James "articulate." Why would she trust you? I bet you barely know anything about her. You barely know anything about *me*, and we get drinks every two weeks."

It was spilling out of me without thought, and I saw Owen shrinking. His face was flushing. I thought there was a chance he'd blow up on me, but he went the opposite direction. He got small and fragile. I kept going.

"Like, I don't even work for you, and you try to poke me about being Black. I can't imagine what it's like to work at your company. It's probably terrible for her there." I stopped. I could see he was embarrassed, and Brett was leaning his body away from the table to avoid catching any strays. It was quiet for a beat, just the sound of the blaring, ridiculous bar music.

Hey, I just met you!

And this is crazy!

But here's my number!

So call me, maybe!

Owen finally spoke, but he was hunched and looked wounded. His voice came out soft and quivering in a way I'd never heard from him. All of his domineering bravado was gone for now.

"Jesus, dude." He took a breath. "Wow." I had so much space in the conversation, more than I'd ever felt with these two guys. For the first time, it felt like *I* had the power in our dynamic. But I just let the space sit there while Owen processed.

"Do you really think so?" Owen asked. He was giving me a chance to be a coward again. He was giving me a chance to back off of what I was asserting, that he was someone Black people could not and should not trust. He pleaded with his eyes for me to walk back from what I'd said. And I went the opposite direction.

"I do. Shit, I wouldn't wanna be in her seat," I responded. At this point I had no idea what would come next. I was out in deep waters well beyond any point I'd crossed with white people before, especially white people I was trying to do business with. So what came next surprised me.

For the first time, Owen asked me an earnest question. I had found a vulnerability that Owen seemed already aware of, and now he wanted help.

"Man, that's really honest of you to share that. What do you think I could do differently?" he asked me. I was so surprised. I thought, wow, how the dynamic has shifted. We were at eye level, and Owen was asking *me* for help.

I was uncorked, and I had so much to say on this topic. I drew from my experiences at Google and at my new employer and all of my dinners and drinks and baseball games with white execs like Owen to give what I thought was a comprehensive point of view on how people like Owen could make life less difficult for people like Sydney and me. Owen was engaged and curious and kept asking more questions. I kept giving answers. Brett started to join in. They gave me a sort of eye contact I had never felt from white people. They seemed to really see me and hear me.

And I got my first hit of a drug, white deference, that would hook me. And *all* it took to get it was for me to open my mouth and be honest about race. *What a perfect exchange*, I thought.

The next day, I got a text from Owen thanking me for my candor. He told me that it took a real friend to be honest about such a difficult topic. I glowed in his admiration. A week or so later, I received an email from Owen, with Brett cc'd, requesting a contract for partnership. They were ready to pay to come on as our first official partnering client, and they were going to send us a check upon signature. I remember reading the email and laughing out loud alone in my office.

I told white people my truth about race, and not only did it draw them *nearer*, now they were giving me money. I carried this truth-telling about race into my journaling and notes, and then into my conversations with white people at work and in my life outside of work—and I watched many of them respond the same way Owen and Brett did.

Curious. Stammering. Deferential.

A couple months later, I opened a Google doc and began writing a book proposal for what would become my first book: *Black Magic: What Black Leaders Learned from Trauma and Triumph*. I was going to write and publish a book about my Black experiences and how I and others used our Black traumas to excel.

I was going to sell Black stories for money. I had seen in a short time the size of the return on this exchange in my social and professional life, and I wanted more of the money especially. It seemed like a win-win: The book could offer tools and tactics to Black achievers while simultaneously gaining me deference and money from white audiences.

I thought I had found a gold mine that would cost me very little to access.

I had the unlimited resource: lived experience as a Black person. I could use it as I pleased. I could open the vault and trade my point of view to get rich. When I so chose. I was in the power seat now. I was in control.

Boy, was I fucking wrong.

What I gave Owen and Brett at that table was a diversity and inclusion consultation. Despite Owen's behavior that I often felt to be brazen microaggressions, misogyny, and outright racism, he was what many would describe as a well-meaning, white, liberal tech CEO. Part of his identity was being *one of the good guys*. An *ally*. He self-imposed hiring quotas on his company to ensure that their workforce was more diverse than the rest of the woefully monoculture tech industry. He invested tens of thousands of dollars each year from his company's budget to sponsor big-name tech diversity and inclusion conferences throughout the year. He was savvy enough to arrange his company's "Meet the Team" web page alphabetically, burying him and Brett, whose last names started with *S* and *T*, respectively, so that a few of the employees with Black and brown faces would be visible higher up on the pages for anyone scrolling through. It was a manipulative move to organize the site that way, showing off token diversity, but Owen was already sensitive to the snowballing industrial diversity and inclusion pseudo-reckoning that would hit an inflection point in the summer of 2020. And he was wise to bend his image to make himself appear to be someone Black people could feel safe working under. A kind master, if you will.

But he wasn't *actually* safe. Underneath it all was still someone who thought Black people (and women, and other people of color) were beneath him. He wanted so badly for his facade to be perfect. He knew himself and his underlying toxins, but he wanted those toxins to be invisible. He wanted to know for sure that even someone with the keenest eye for an imposter couldn't clock him as a faux ally. I suspect he wanted that because it made him feel good, and also because it made him look good and ahead of the curve to the people he valued most: other white people. Hence the extra-long hug with the Black bouncer at the otherwise entirely white bar. Hence the enormous checks to put his company's name beside the names of other companies with white leadership sponsoring D&I tech conferences. And hence . . . me . . . sitting beside him for drinks every few weeks.

His performance of closeness and casualness with me in front of Brett gave him the ultimate edge over someone with whom he had to share his leadership title: co-CEO. And he leaned further and further into his show of comfort with me, all the way into pulling his juvenile ribbing bullshit with me in a way that revealed his casual racism. *Dat asssssssssss.*

And by confronting him on said bullshit, I had revealed myself as an asset. His transformation into the master ally was incomplete, and now he knew it because I had pointed out its imperfections. I remember his gaze, so attentive and focused as I walked out each of the ways I saw him as a danger to Sydney, his Black employee. He wasn't listening because he wanted to learn how to be a better person, but because he wanted to learn how to *seem* like one.

For once, he was listening, *actually listening*, to me because I could help him complete his facade. He was finally seeing value in me.

It wasn't the value I had hoped he'd see, as a business partner. It was more the value of a mirror. I was showing him where he needed to improve his act so that when CEOs and execs started getting fired more frequently for being racist, he'd be safe. And wouldn't you know it, what I got in return was the thing I'd been after all along: his money.*

I got such a high from our exchange, our *trade*. I felt so powerful having his full attention in that conversation. And then I felt euphoric when I saw his offer of money and partnership. I thought of myself as a swashbuckling closer. And *all* it took was leaning into my Blackness and telling a white person about himself. A trade-off crystallized in my head. I could do this for money—tell the truth about my racial experience and cash checks.

A few years later, George Floyd was murdered by the police, Black people and others protested, and the moment for which Owen had been readying himself arrived. White liberals and executives and managers and companies everywhere were in a crazed and urgent rush to protect themselves from the backlash of the moment by washing themselves with a facade of allyship. They were ready to spend money to plunge into the waters of whatever would make them look like they truly cared about what Black people were so heartbroken and enraged about. And I just so happened to be publishing a book about the tools and tactics that many Black leaders had used to thrive in an anti-Black country. The tragedies of the moment created a waiting audience for my book. In the tech world, this phenomenon is known as product-market fit.

---

* I've since gotten updates from mutual colleagues on Owen, and I know he never changed the things he said to people at bars, or how he manipulated people who worked for him. And yet, he's been celebrated in the tech industry for his allyship. I've heard he's even writing a book about it.

I urged my publisher to push up the release of my book, and on February 2, 2021, Black History Month, just months after the Summer of George Floyd, *Black Magic* was published into a feeding frenzy for stories about Black trauma and how people and companies could respond to it. People like Brené Brown and Dax Shepard invited me on their enormous podcast platforms to talk about anti-Blackness in corporations and society. Julie Bowen, of *Modern Family* fame, reached out to me to explore ways to work together. (For the record, all three of those people became friends of mine and champions of my work.)

Thousands of white people, mostly women from middle America, followed me on Instagram. I got a second book deal, for the book you're reading now, even before my first book came out. Audible, Amazon's audiobook and podcasting platform, gave me a large deal to publish an eight-part series called *Direct Deposit*, exploring the complications that arise in Black people's lives as we ascend in our careers. Giant companies with white leadership like Google and Target gave me money to come speak to their teams about what they could do to make life more comfortable for their Black employees at work.

I was hardly an expert. I didn't have a master's or PhD in African American Studies or Corporate Human Resources. All I had done was write about how difficult it is to be Black in America. I spoke directly to the anti-Black warts in corporate America. It was the same thing I'd done with Owen. And in return white people were celebrating me and throwing money at me to be a mirror for them just like Owen had. *What a simple exchange*, I thought. *I could do this forever. This will make me rich!*

In December 2022, just a few years later, I sat by my firepit in my backyard in Queens wondering how I'd become so unhappy. So much of what I'd hustled and prayed for during my transition from Tech-Boy-Genius-Wannabe to aspiring creative had come true. I was creating in every format—TV, podcasting, print—and my name was buzzing. I was making good money from the very trade-off I had been so eager to plunge myself into. I was writing and speaking and podcasting about anti-Blackness and how difficult it can be to endure white supremacy in this country. And I was making damn good money for it. And I was a misery.

Every day I probed myself for race traumas, crafted them into art, and traded them off for money and attention. I thought the trade-off would be worthwhile because I thought being rich would make me happy. I thought I could buy what I always wanted, *freedom*. But I hadn't taken the time to think about what freedom really was. I hadn't known that I'd be giving away all of my mental freedom in freedom's pursuit. To write and publish race trauma is to live and re-live inside a barrel of darkness. Writing doesn't just happen at the keyboard. It happens in the shower, thinking about that time you got arrested and thought the cop might shoot you. It happens at the dinner table with your family, rewording that sentence in your head about the white person at the gas station window who locked the doors just as you approached to pay in freezing cold weather. It happens when your fiancée is asking you, begging you, to be more present but you're busy thinking about the right tonal balance in your voice to convey your hissing anger in a way that is palatable enough to white people.

Not to mention all those corporate speaking gigs about race—staring at a Zoom screen and trying to force my way into practical answers to impractical questions.

How can Company XYZ make itself a place where Black employees feel happy to work? "You can't. You'll never know if your Black employees feel happy to work for you. They'll never tell you the truth. They can't trust you."

How can Company XYZ improve its diversity hiring efforts?

"By starting at the top. Remove two of your white board members and replace them with Black ones. But c'mon. You'll never do that."

How did it feel for you to work at Google? How did it feel to leave?

"Working there felt like suffocating alone, dying quietly inside, while everyone surrounded you, yelling at you, demanding that you be happy. Leaving felt like breathing air for the first time."

I felt myself and my answers get darker. I realized that giving them what they wanted, the facade of looking like they cared about their Black employees, meant that I had to lie. And I didn't leave corporate America just to be paid to do whatever they said, same as I had while working in corporate America. So even that part of my life, speaking to audiences, something that I have a gift for and usually enjoy, became a dread for me.

I walked around my life sensitive and angry and volatile and reactive because I was living in the most grotesque armpit of our country's conversations: race relations. My natural humor and levity were dying. I could only make jokes that poked at white people. I took jabs from my Black friends and family more personally because I was constantly in a defensive crouch from working on Black-centered projects with white and non-Black execs and producers every day. I got into yelling matches at work with these partners because I felt the weight of being "the Black voice" and needing to stand up *for* a Black point of view—mine—that I sometimes confused as *the* Black point of view.

I was depleting creatively, and inside I felt like burnt cigarette ashes, but I was willing to live in this fog as long as people kept giving me money. And I was willing to endure my growing reputation as an asshole, and someone who is difficult to work with, because I thought maybe that was the price I had to pay to get my point of view into my projects, unsanitized. I was willing to make this trade-off—misery for money—because I'm a storyteller and a performer.

As a storyteller, it was easy for me to tell myself that what I was feeling wasn't unhealthy, it wasn't pain. It was simply struggle. It was the struggle that would result in my enormous, ego-inflating victory, where I'd surface on the other side as a rich, Black storyteller who could choose to leave trauma art behind whenever he chose. All I needed to do was get through a few years of trading my race traumas for money. What a story that would be. And how dare I circumvent it to feel happy in the present?

It was a convenient story, but there was a complication. Other people close to me might be able to tell that the work I was doing was putting me in a bad place. They might warn me off of it, or check in with me in a way that made me rethink my trade-off. A few friends and even my mother mentioned that they thought I was being a little testy. The mere mention of that usually led to a blowup between us.

"I'm not being testy! You're testy," I'd say.

"I'm not being aggressive, you just don't like that I'm being honest," was another of my favorites. Or even this ridiculousness:

"I'm not being an asshole. I'm just a New Yorker now."

This created a distance between me and some people I loved. And with that distance, I could continue to live in my little hole of race trauma, giving it the devotion I thought was required to make my art transcend. And if I ever needed something to lie to me and tell me that I was in fact happy, I had Instagram. My new following there to see how I was soaring. I'd post a photo smiling next to one of the celebrities my work had brought into my life—Jamie Foxx, Spike Lee, Julie Bowen, Jimmy Kimmel, Morgan Freeman, Issa Rae—with a caption grounded in my voice to tell people that even though my life was changing, I was still the same. I was unaffected. I was *happy*. After posting the photo, I'd check the likes compulsively to see who was out there believing that I was happy. Now I, like Owen, was only looking for mirrors to tell me that I was killing it. To tell me that my performance of success and joy was not only convincing, but resonating.

My isolation within this house of mirrors was almost complete. It was almost perfect. But there was one person left whom I hadn't fully pushed away, and from whom I couldn't hide behind a phone screen. That was my then fiancée.

Jules is a native New Yorker from Hollis, Queens. She is the daughter of Dominican and Cuban immigrants. She's *very* tough, and very discerning. She can see. And she is not one for gaslighting.

She never contested how *much* I was working. She too is a worker bee and a successful entrepreneur in her own right. But she saw clearly how unhappy I was in my hole, and she wasn't willing to live her life unhappy with me. My demeanor had to change. She required it. She started off by making light suggestions that I find things besides work that make me happy. She suggested we find new ways to have fun—traveling, trying new things in the city, going out dancing more often. And we tried those ideas, but I took my swirling thoughts about race traumas with me. I wasn't there with her. I was in my hole. And I could turn any fun or easy moment into a cranky argument because cranky arguments had become me. Such is life when your job is telling people how hard it is to be Black, people who don't want to believe it.

Jules insisted that I find a way to enjoy life so that *we* could enjoy life together, and I set out on the mission of trying to be happy while also trying to do this job as the guy who writes and talks about race. I said it before—the money was good and it was getting better. I tried so many ways to trick myself into thinking I could be happy while doing that job. But every time, Jules was there, the worst kind of mirror for someone trying to lie to himself. The honest kind.

And so I find myself in the middle of a tug-of-war between two poles that are diametrically opposed. There is the side that follows the money, and takes the check, and the next check, to write, talk, and create around Black suffering. That side continues to license its voice to white people looking for ways to make themselves appear to care about Black suffering. And on the other side there is freedom, relief from the joyless role of Black trauma storyteller. On that side, I climb out of the hole and leave behind the gold coins stacked inside it.

The side of happiness comes with unknown risk. How will I make a living? Do I have anything to say beyond my commentary on race? Do I have the talent and the savvy to succeed in other forms of art?

I have to bet yes. Because the risk of continuing on down the path that I started when I sat down with Owen and Brett in 2016 *will certainly* destroy me. It's already begun to do so.

The pages that follow detail my experiences navigating the fraught relationships between Blackness, money, trauma sales, and freedom. These stories begin just at the time in my life when I consciously started to parse these concepts and when I learned that I could trade them for each other. Many of these moments were painful to experience; they were painful again to write about. That's a trade-off I can't keep making.

And so, this is my last time writing about race.

2

Get Out of Jail Free

A few years before I met Owen and Brett, I had already begun to experiment with the theory that money and a fancy job title could build my self-esteem and give me a voice. I was working at Google in the human resources department as a lowly "Level 2," which is dehumanizing Google-speak for "entry level associate." Like many (or most) corporate tech employees, I was encouraged by my employer to think of myself as lucky to work at a company that gave me money and health insurance and occasional team dinners and company off-sites in exchange for the majority of my available thoughts, energy, and time spent on earth. As a Black employee I paid an additional tax of frequent microaggressions and looming anxiety about whether or not I was "Googly" enough, an actual graded performance metric at the time. Even so, I was willing to trade most of my existence for corporate asylum and bonuses and free lunch with my eyes wide open for an important unstated benefit: confidence. Or something like it.

I was an insecure early twentysomething. At each stage of life, I had wrapped myself around an identity that could numb the shaky feeling of not knowing whether I mattered, or more honestly, knowing that I didn't. As a naïve elementary school student, I slid easily into the costume of being the "smart Black kid," which might as well have been my name among the white and Asian kids in my gifted and talented classes in Montgomery County, Maryland.

In middle school, basketball offered me an identity that gave me closeness to the other Black kids at school and made me feel like something cooler and more human than an anomalous token for white kids to marvel at. Basketball gave me a feeling of value, both among my peers and the men in my family who loved sports, and I clung to the scaffolding of cocky sneering athlete all the way up until the beginning of my senior year when I had to face the truth: The market for 5'8.5" combo guards at the Division 1 level was virtually nonexistent.

When I got to Morehouse College in Atlanta, I felt the soft, soothing calm of belonging for the first time in the Atlanta University Center. I was in a sea of young, curious, explorative Black people like me. But soon I felt *too* much belonging. Without my roles as token or athlete, I felt like there was nothing that made me stand out.

And so I did what men in college frequently do when they feel unexceptional: I joined a fraternity. And boy did I go all in. The exclusivity and flamboyance of fraternity life gave me a potent jolt of contrived confidence, and it flooded my veins so corrosively that I began to mistake it for *real* confidence, like the kind I had felt playing sports throughout my life. I gulped down fake confidence like wine from a goblet. I got a tattoo with the Greek letters of my fraternity on my shoulder blade. I wore dog tags emblazoned with my fraternity's emblem around my neck to announce to anyone who met me that I belonged to something that gave me meaning and status. I played the role of frat boy until I began to be known as Chad the Alpha. And I relished that title, totally oblivious to the shame that it is to only be worth knowing for my proximity to a larger group of people. I had no time to consider *why* I wanted to be known as something bigger or more noteworthy than just . . . myself. I had no time for introspection at all. I had toga parties to throw.

And then I graduated, moved to Oakland to start my job at Google's headquarters in Mountain View, California, and noticed that all my confidence cloaks were gone. I was naked again. At Google I wasn't the "smart Black kid"—most people there were smart. I wasn't an athlete. I wasn't a frat boy. I was just a Level 2.

But I noticed that *outside* of Google headquarters, it meant something to people that I worked at *the world's greatest place to work.* I noticed people's ears prick up when I told them about my job, and I laid it on thick, trying to keep them engaged so I could absorb their adulation for my ever-needy ego. I made Google, a place that made me feel small and inadequate, sound like some lush utopia of cargo shorts and Warby Parker glasses.

You know, it just does something for your spirit when you're working hard all day and you look over and see a Labrador retriever puppy. Every company should have a bring-your-dog-to-work day.

I don't think of my coworkers as coworkers, so much as I think of them as . . . friends. You know? That's how it should be.

I don't even know how much money I'm making this year. Honestly? I would work at a place like this for free.

I needed whoever I was talking to—at a restaurant, at a friend's birthday, at a bar—to think that what I did and what I belonged to said something grand about who I was. If I could get them to believe it, maybe I could believe it. If I could convince them, maybe I could convince myself. Maybe I could forget that I hated where I worked.

Like I said, as a storyteller, it's not all that difficult to convince yourself of something untrue. But if it ever becomes difficult, drinking helps.

In the summer of 2013, just a few months after my twenty-fifth birthday, I awoke at a stoplight with my foot on the brake pedal of my mother's Nissan Altima in Bethesda, Maryland. It was late into the a.m. hours of the night, and I should have been startled by the few cars whizzing by, but I was more rattled by the knocking on my driver's-side window.

A stout white police officer with a buzz cut and serious, tired eyes was tapping very forcefully on my driver's-side window and instructing, no, commanding me to put the car in park and get out slowly. I tensed then released, understanding at once that I was under the cop's power until he told me otherwise. Even with my blood alcohol level well above the legal limit, I could recall my father's lessons on how to survive an encounter with police. I did exactly as I was told, however woozy.

My body relaxed, and I became a marionette to the buzz-cut cop's voice. Once I was fully out of the vehicle, he fervently searched my body—for weapons or drugs, I guessed. Then he directed me through a sequence of aerobic demonstrations to judge my drunkenness while his partner—taller and goofier—watched on from eight or so feet away.

The sobriety test I most remember, really the only one I remember, was one in which he had me try to walk along a straight line painted on the ground: one foot in front of the other, heel to toe, heel to toe. The police car's bright headlights cast shadows of my slight, twenty-five-year-old Black body trying to walk the line. I remember thinking, as adrenaline sobered me, that even this small exercise was a chance to get a passing grade from the two white police officers. I almost relished this unexpected opportunity to impress someone by passing a test on this quiet Bethesda side street under the unsupervised purview of two white male cops in the middle of the night.

The booze helped ease my nerves. Alcohol was my suppressant of choice then. It was what I used to build a fortress of counterfeit confidence; confidence I needed to laugh along to lazy, condescending jokes at my own expense at work happy hours; confidence I needed to live in New York City, a loud, tall, expensive city that bludgeons everyone, but especially gouges those without means. A beer and a shot offered me a simulacrum of the confidence I needed to go back into the office and ignore how lonely I was.

And so, with that liquid poise still seeping out my pores, I thought I would do The Walk perfectly, and I'd then look at the cops, they'd smile, make a joke, and send me on my way. I would get an A+. I was still working at Google then. I was a good boy with my neat Caesar haircut and closet full of short-sleeved button-ups. I knew, I thought, how to get a passing grade on any inane exercise. I was palatable. Surely, they'd see that and set me on my way.

I tried The Walk. I stumbled on each attempt. I never actually hit the ground, but I came close.

I failed. This was one of my many failures that night.

The next thing I knew I was sitting in the back of the police car, staring at the back of the buzz-cut cop's head through the partition as he drove us along. I was handcuffed. Yes, just like the movies.

The cuffs were tight, but they weren't going to injure me. I remember wondering if I could slip out of them. It was just something to think about as we drove. I would never actually try that. I was a good boy. I remember thinking there was something cool and interesting about wearing *real* handcuffs. I was scared, of course. Mostly scared of how this was going to hurt my family. I was scared that I was going to lose my job if I was charged with a DUI. I didn't know the rules around those things.

The drive to jail was short. Or it was long. I don't remember. But my next memory was sitting in the jail office, handcuffed to a chair that was mounted to the floor. The tall cop sat next to me for a chat while the more serious, buzz-cut cop did paperwork and all the important stuff. The tall cop was sweeter. It was really like a good cop, bad cop routine. The tall cop felt familiar, like the father of a white kid I might have played high school basketball against at Wootton High School or Bethesda–Chevy Chase. Those were the schools on the other side of the county where the *really* white families lived. Those kids' parents were reasonably polite at the games. They were less welcoming if you showed up at their door for a house party.

I told the tall cop this was my first arrest. He didn't seem surprised. I could tell he already had labeled me as a "good boy." A "good kid," maybe. He kept asking questions, and I kept opening up, giving him exactly what he wanted. I know how to be charming to white people when I need to, but back then I was practicing daily and at the top of my game. I *really* knew how to lay it on. At some point he opened the door for me to tell him that I worked at Google.

That meant something to him.

This was 2013. Google was named *Fortune*'s #1 Best Company to Work For that year. It was one of Google's four consecutive years at the top of that list. The tall cop knew the company's reputation. He smiled more. He asked me what it was like to work there. He insinuated that I must be well compensated working there, even as a twenty-five-year-old, an age he knew for certain from having confiscated my license.

I gave him everything he could hope for in the conversation. He had college-aged kids. He hoped they would get a job at a place like Google when they graduated. At that time, parents of young people around my age were always casually, not-so-subtly telling me that they wished their kids could get a job at Google—as if *I* could hire them. Some would just send me their adult child's résumé with a subject line reading "Do you think Google might have a place for Ralphy?"

But this was—and is—the dance of prestige. Of promise. Of money, or the whiff of money. I performed for the cop. I told him about all the wonderful things I'd seen at the company. I told him about puppy dogs walking through the clean, clipped gardens between cafeterias full of free gourmet food. I told him about my generous stock options and how I, in my mid-twenties, could afford to live in SoHo with a roommate who was a junior investment banker at Goldman Sachs. I told him that the Mountain View office was cool, the one he'd seen in movies like *The Internship* and on TV. But oh, he should see the New York office. So posh, so expansive, taking up an entire city block in Manhattan's Chelsea neighborhood. I told him how I used to walk there when I lived on Christopher Street, paying $2,800 per month for one room in a two-bedroom, and how *that* was a bargain. But oh, I had to move because the parades that came down West Fourth Street and Broadway were just too much.

He was taken. He was enthralled, or at least he seemed to be. I watched him thaw, become even kinder. I tried to give him exactly the experience he wanted. I created the mirage of a young, charming, Black, rich tech executive on his way up the ladder, living in sexy Manhattan—as best I could while chained to a chair.

While the tall cop melted, the buzz-cut cop mostly ignored me. He focused on the paperwork and eventually interrupted my performance. He would not be wooed, and I knew that from the first moment I saw his posture and heavy eyes bearing down on me from outside my mother's car window.

Buzz-cut cop informed me of the blood alcohol level I had revealed by blowing into the Breathalyzer. I was way too intoxicated to be driving a car. He told me some things about the next steps of my arrest. He told me where my car would be impounded. I think he gave me back my wallet, *sans* license, because my next memory is out of body. It's a vision of myself, in a minivan taxi with the sun starting to show itself, on my way to my parents' house in Silver Spring. I was not handcuffed anymore, so I had no reason to woo the taxi driver.

The ride was around thirty minutes long. Long enough for the shame, and darkness, and gravity of my failure to fishhook in my stomach. Let me be specific about those failures. My dad shared many principles with me throughout childhood, but the one that stuck, above all others, the one I meant to become a purpose, was this: "Never let anyone take away your freedom."

He would say it in the most unexpected moments when I was five, when I was nine, when I was thirteen. He would say it when I got home from basketball practice. He would say it in the car if we heard a story on the radio about someone receiving a long prison sentence. He would say it as we passed the drug addicted and houseless on East Capitol Street in Washington, DC, on the way to see relatives.

"Never let anyone take away your freedom."

He would say it with a calm, almost joy, on his face. He would kind of squint his eyes and smile when he said it. Like a cat enjoying a sunny spot in the room.

"Never let anyone take away your freedom."

As a kid I would poke at the statement, checking for weakness in its foundation. I was testing it. He seemed so sure those words were the way. I wanted to be sure.

"What if that means I have to commit a crime? Or break out of jail?" I'd ask, thinking I'd finally cornered him. He'd just smile and repeat the words back to me, just as easy and sturdy as before.

"Never let anyone take away your freedom."

He never forced the statement. It would pass through him to me like a breeze. I liked when he said it. I liked how he said it. It implied that I already had freedom, and I only needed to protect it or to engage it or to know that it was there.

But it also implied that someone might try to take it, or worse, that I might willingly give it away. On that night I had failed that precious mission. Thirty minutes earlier, I was chained to a chair while two cops took away my license—my identity—and filed me into the dreaded system. Before that I was cuffed in the back of their vehicle. Before that I was asleep in the driver's seat of an ignited vehicle at a stoplight. I could have been killed. I could have killed someone.

But a few hours before that, I was at a bar, with my Google ID hanging from my chinos hoping for all to see and some to inquire, buying round after round after round of shots for a distant friend from my high school and her friends and their friends. Most were white.

They were strangers, save for a couple of people. And yet I kept ordering shots, and handing them out, and downing them, and ordering more. Some strangers left, new strangers replaced them, and I kept buying shots and flashing that 6 x 4 laminated Google badge.

Why did I want them to see my Google badge? Why did I want to spend $330 on drinks for them? Because I wanted them to think I was attractive. I wanted them to think I was adequate. But most of all, if all else failed, I wanted them to think I was rich.

I walked back to my car alone after all those conversations with faceless strangers and countless shots and an absurd amount of money spent. I don't remember a face in the crowd except for Suzie's. I don't remember a word that was said. I don't think I've seen any of those people since. When the bar closed down around me, I walked alone to a diner and took a nap on the table. When the diner closed, I walked to my car and took another nap in the parking garage. From there, I drove out of the parking structure to what I guess was the first or second stoplight on the way to the highway. And, well, I guess I went ahead and took another nap there.

And when the buzz-cut cop tapped on my glass, I knew I had failed the mission. My freedom was taken away. I gave it away.

But in truth, I'd given it away well before that when I allowed my life's purpose, my mission, my identity, my sense of self, my sense of adequacy to be ruled mercilessly by my pursuit of money.

The next morning I missed breakfast because I had gotten in so late. My mother had already left to go meet my older sister at her new home. I had traveled down from New York for the weekend to be with my family and celebrate her buying her first condo. The irony was not lost on me then, and it stays with me now: On a weekend in which my sister was marking a milestone of estate building and potential wealth creation for our family, I had risked flushing my "good job" down the drain and exposed myself to expensive court proceedings and legal processes. In other words, while my sister was doing something great, I had done something destructive and shortsighted. But that didn't really hurt. Not yet.

The next part hurt. I walked into the garage where my dad was impatiently waiting for me to wake up and get ready to join my mom and sister. My dad was pretty stern when I was a kid, but since I've been an adult he is pleasant and happy to see me when we get together. But today he looked at me like an insubordinate, pathetic kid. Today he looked at me like I had failed him, or myself, or everyone. I had.

"Where's your mother's car?" he asked me with gravelly tension in his voice. His eyes fixed on me, telling me to be still and honest.

I did as his eyes instructed.

"I, uh . . . It's at an impound lot," I said, weak and ashamed.

"Why?" he said.

"I got a DUI last night," I replied.

What he said next I will never forget.

"Chad, I already did this with your grandfather. I'm not doing it with you."

Drinking as a means for fake confidence loosened its grip on me in that moment. The grip of money as a pursuit, as a purpose, only tightened in the years that followed. I'm still chained to it like the chair in that Montgomery County jail. I want to be free. Maybe this book will help.

3

Buffoonery and Violence

I have a fear I don't speak or write about much. I'm afraid that nobody wants to read a book written by a happy Black person. I recently entered a phase of joy. I am in it now. I'm not rich. I'm not famous. But I love most of my life right now. I live in Queens in a place that is spacious by New York standards. I have a three-year-old German shepherd who bounces and whines to make sure we get outside for an adventure every day. I have good friends nearby, in Brooklyn, who cook sliders on football Sundays. We listen to music and rib each other and laugh and play cards. I play basketball on Tuesday nights and feel what it's like to compete and connect with other guys in their thirties who still think they can hoop. I work with a small, hungry team of creatives on podcasts and TV series and digital media. We see each other. We inspire each other. Every couple months I get to see my three adorable nephews who live in Maryland, in the house I lived in at their age.

I explore New York. I eat, I date, I create, I wander, I hustle, I rest. New York is a chaotic mess, but it's a good life. On days like today I wake up around eight a.m. with my heart light and beating quickly. I'm excited for the day.

Penny is on all fours eating breakfast from her bowl. When she's done, I take her out the back door into the yard. I chase her around for ten minutes to get the puppy energy out before our walk. We exit the back gate, and we're right in the concrete center of Queens. There's asphalt and trash on the ground. There's a large graveyard to the right, not even a block away from our house. A sign in front of the cemetery reads DEAD END.

Penny is pulling at her leash, excited to go on our adventure. I think to myself how lucky I am to get to wander and think my own thoughts with my puppy. We make our way out onto Myrtle Avenue, and I notice the few trees scattered across the gray, urban landscape. Our forest is dirty and there's trash everywhere. But we're happy. We're outside and nobody can tell us what to do. When I worked in the giant, ugly office buildings in Manhattan, I felt chained down. When I quit that life for creative industries, I spent most of my time trying to find ways to make money to pay my bills. That chase consumed me, preventing me from feeling free. I felt the intruding impulse to check my phone to see if an agent had called me back or if one of my projects had officially been cut by a studio. I felt intrusive voices in my head telling me everything I had to do differently and everyone I had to be to have a chance to make it in "Hollywood"—a place I still have never lived.

Those voices controlled me. They told me I had to move more urgently, more desperately, to beat out the other writers who all wanted to sell TV shows and land writers' room jobs like I did. They were the voices of managers, business managers, lawyers, agents, studio executives, ex-friends, and some family members. They were invasive. They were authoritative. They said, "You have to do this if you want that." They assumed they knew what I wanted. They assumed they knew how to get those things.

What I wanted was expression, audience, freedom. They had none of those things, and never knew how to get them. They were frauds. What underpinned their advice most of all was the assumption that I wanted *money*. Who doesn't? They poked at my insecurity around not having money and my fear of never making money. That was their leverage to tell me who I was. *If you never do this, you will just be another broke Black person.* I obeyed.

But now, on my walk with Penny, I can only hear those voices if I try to evoke them. I ignore them. In a material way, I ignore their calls and texts when they don't serve me. Because what's important right now is going on a walk around Queens with my puppy. Wandering. Imagining. Thinking of what I want to do next and who I want to be.

When I get home, I'll listen to music in the kitchen, and when I feel moved, I'll make my way into the office. I'll set the studio lights in my office to give a blue hue. Or maybe pink or purple. Whatever I'm feeling today. I'll open my phone, my computer, and a notebook. I'll review the thoughts I've scribbled out over the past twenty-four hours and decide what I want to write. I know what I write will reach thousands, at least, who will judge it and project their own meaning onto it. That's the point. I try not to let that cloud what I say, but it's nice to know my voice will reach people. It's so frustrating to pour into writing that never sees daylight because the process requires exorcizing buried feelings; it can be painful to drag them back out into the light of day.

When it's time to procrastinate, I open Instagram and check my DMs. A stranger in Atlanta listened to my podcast and shared it with her best friend who just quit her job at Facebook and needs inspiration. Another stranger in Chicago read my first book and cried because he was fired for being a big Black man, called a "non-culture-fit" at a tech startup. These people are telling me that my work moved them and that I should keep going.

So I keep going.

When I finish writing I close the computer and take a ride around the corner to El Mekkah—a smoky hookah bar in Bushwick where they play the games on big TVs and a mix of hip-hop and afrobeats on the painfully loud stereo. I chat with the bartender and a couple of the other patrons who are checking in from varied New York lives. One works at the post office. Another works at Island Records. Another is recording her first album and she's nervous and brimming with excitement. My phone buzzes, and it's my sister. I'll call her back; we talk every day. It buzzes again, and it's my agent calling to schedule a Netflix pitch. I'll call her back too.

I watch the Brooklyn Nets dart up and down the court and zone out, thinking how lucky I am to get to choose who I want to be; reflecting on how desperate, and afraid, and chasing I have felt for the last few years. My neck tenses scrolling through it all in my head. Then the bartender places a vanilla blueberry hookah in front of me and shakes me out of my memories. I feel cool relief to be back in the life I have today.

On the car ride home I drive through Brooklyn and then Queens in silence. I am free for a moment.

But when I walk back into my place, I plop on my couch and turn on the TV without thinking. Muscle memory. I scroll through the streaming services on the TV. I see the titles and their marketing. You know the names—I won't list them here. I know the people who make these shows. I know their bosses. I run into them. I'm on calls with them. I respect them, but I wonder how they can live with the Hollywood-filtered versions of their art. Or maybe I'm jealous of them. Maybe I want my own show, in my voice, and who cares if it's run through the same bastardizing Hollywood filter. Maybe I want the executive producer and creator fees that come with it.

And then fear arrives.

In the last three years I have experienced success writing candidly about underexposed emotional dimensions of Black struggle. I wrote a viral *New York Times* op-ed called "I Don't Need Love Texts from My White Friends" in the wake of George Floyd's murder. I published a book called *Black Magic* about tactics and strategies learned through pain. I executive produced and hosted an Audible Originals podcast called *Direct Deposit* exploring the ropes course Black people face trying to build our fortunes.

The latter two projects were emotionally difficult to write. When I'm writing something over months or years, I spend much of my time in the moments that comprise the story. And so, when I'm writing something that deals with my experiences and other people's experiences with anti-Blackness, I live with those feelings while creating. I feel my body tense up. I feel it in my chest. I feel the pressure in my forehead when I leave the work and see white people in my life, in my neighborhood. I brace myself. I don't sleep well. Some writers, I guess, are able to better compartmentalize their emotions when writing. I haven't yet developed that skill. Or maybe they're just better at hiding the pain.

One might ask, well then why write about Black struggle? The first answer is obvious: Lived experience is the first and most available resource for writers. But the second answer also seems obvious. I feel a market pressure to lean into pain. When I scroll through the list of popular shows centering Black male characters today, I see that the ones that find success—*Snowfall*, *Power*, *Top Boy*, *Godfather of Harlem*—all focus on Black men ruling over violent crime empires.

Donald Glover's *Atlanta* was an exception to the rule, and for several years it was my favorite TV series and a creative North Star. The show featured crime and violence but as part of a larger story told about friendship and aspiration and the complex inner lives within its characters. While watching *Atlanta*, I wasn't subjected to watching brutal, bloody murders and assaults on Black people in every episode as I am when watching other shows that center Black men—even shows I love but can't find the stomach to rewatch, like *The Wire*.

Instead *Atlanta* inspired me with its use of surrealism, slow-burning plotlines and character arcs, and Easter eggs, not to mention its cultural commentary and flat-out punchline laughs. I guffawed when a D'Angelo impersonator in the show made himself a fried chicken skin sandwich. I nodded along through an entire episode devoted to critiquing a facsimile of Tyler Perry's enormous, ham-fisted creative factory in Atlanta. I loved watching the show's main character, Earn, face conflict with his girlfriend, Van, and best friends, Alfred and Darius, without dehumanizing one another. There were fights and bickering and bumping egos and neglected duties of fatherhood and friendship, but these friends never caused serious harm to each other. There was no violent shootout between Earn and Alfred. Van never plotted with Darius to steal from Earn. They were just a group of friends trying to uphold their connections to one another while pursuing their individual needs in a confusing world. I could relate. And I still got my fill of rapper cameos and a soundtrack filled with 808s; the world *Atlanta* built never felt detached altogether from this one that I live in.

I don't preside over a drug empire. I don't live in a mansion with cocaine packed in the walls. To feel seen, I sometimes need to watch a show about average Black people just doing life. There's enough drama in day-to-day life for us that it need not be sensationalized, only crafted, to make good television. *Atlanta* accomplished that. But to get it made,

Glover had to pretend it was something else. Not something violent and dark, but something silly.

"I knew what FX wanted from me," Glover told *Complex* magazine in a 2018 interview. "They were thinking it'd be me and Craig Robinson horse-tailing around, and it'll be kind of like *Community*, and it'll be on for a long time. I was Trojan-horsing FX. If I told them what I really wanted to do, it wouldn't have gotten made."

So it seems that if I want to make TV, I'll have to write shows whose characters fall into the studio-accepted buckets of violent gangsters and silly clowns—*or* I'll have to trick the studios with material that reads as such and then sidewind my show into its true premise. It took an Emmy- and Grammy-winning megastar auteur like Donald Glover to pull off the latter. So let's suppose I go for the former, to write violence or clowning. In my experience I've had to live in the world of whatever I'm writing for as long as I'm writing it, and beyond.

When I wrote for *Rap Sh!t* I learned and thought more about emerging rappers, streaming services, Miami scammers, Little Haiti, City Girls, clubs, and DJs than I ever thought I could. I found myself listening to more hip-hop and consuming more rap-related content like *The Breakfast Club*, *The Joe Budden Podcast*, *Million Dollaz Worth of Game*, and *Caresha Please*. I'm not writing on *Rap Sh!t* anymore, but I still watch those shows. The hosts and the guests and the topics of conversation are still in my life and in my mind. I'm incapable of compartmentalizing. I don't have that sort of power over my subconscious.

When I produced *Direct Deposit*, I lost hundreds of hours of sleep over a year treading through my feelings about my experience as a patient to a white therapist, racism in corporate culture, the isolation I feel in career ascendence, and the like. The emotional stress caused by living in that subject matter and discussing and debating it with my production team loomed over me for the entire year. I was constantly on edge, and it caused a strain to my relationships outside my work.

I don't have a taste for buffoonery, and I don't enjoy slapstick comedy, so to write a story about "horse-tailing" around is off the table for me. That leaves me with Black violence if I want the studios to green-light my work. But if I write a show about Black violence, it means I will have to live in Black violence. I will have to watch it. I will have to invent it in my mind. I'll have to describe characters shooting, stabbing, falling, dying. And as a Black person in my thirties, I have already done so much learning about Black violence, and learning how to evade its looming presence, and watching it destroy people I care about, and trying to build a wall of toughness so that thinking about it and fearing it doesn't own me. So plunging into writing a show that features Black violence so the studios will make space for me feels like a threat to my mental health, if not my physical health. Because I'll have to be consumed by crafting and exploring and thinking about Black violence to do it justice.

Regardless of genre or shape of story there's something I have to say. Something about being human while being "Black" and the trades and allowances we have to make to be both at once. Does that sound murky when read on the page? Of course it does. Which is why TV is a better medium for this particular message. So I've taken these ideas and written them out in the shape of a story to try to push them through the sludge of the Hollywood system. Because there are some things we can better show than we can tell, like the dangers swirling around Black people at the highest levels of industry.

Here and there, certain Black creatives are able to break the molds of what stories are accepted into the Hollywood studio system. I'm just here to tell you, as a mercenary who has been working in this system for almost a decade now, that decision-makers at the top of the big studios mandate that their executive underlings source certain types of Black stories: buffoonery, struggle, violence. This is my understanding as someone who has pitched dozens of projects, dozens of times, across the Hollywood studioscape. Netflix. HBO. Amazon. Hulu. And the like. They want Black clowns and Black killers.

I'm not banging my head against the wall anymore. So here is my violent Black story that includes an important message. I've written it at my own risk. That's a trade I am willing to make for a chance to get my point across in film. You'll find the script in the pages here that follow.

4

THE TOURNAMENT

"Pilot"

Written by
Chad Sanders

NOTE: This pilot opens in four different characters' lives playing out in various parts of New York on the same night.

INT. THE COMEDY CELLAR - MANHATTAN - NIGHT

A nervous, floppy-haired Hipster Dude stands on stage in the smoky, intimate room full of mostly white Manhattanites.

HOST

This next guy. Wow. Really? Wow, okay. Folks, here's Danny Watts.

Confused whispers fill the room. DANNY (forties, Black, Dave Chappelle type) marches to the stage, takes the mic from the host, and stands straight in the spotlight.

The tense crowd breaks into a mix of boos and cheers. The cheers win out. Danny basks. He takes a seat on the stool and patiently cracks open a bottle of whiskey. He's a maestro.

DANNY

Thank you all. I know. Some of y'all didn't think y'all was gonna see me again.

A white Comedy Bro yells from the audience.

MAN (O.S.)

WE MISSED YOU DANNY!

The crowd cheers.

DANNY

Oh, please. What has it been, two years since y'all seen me? My kids looking at y'all niggas like . . . "two years, that ain't shit."

Laughter.

DANNY

Yeah, so y'all canceled me. Just left me out to dry, cold turkey. At least when my side bitches leave they call a few days later to tell me they gave me the clap! But y'all are ruthless! Here today, gone tomorrow.

A few groans, then a wave of laughs and applause. Danny grins and lights a cigarette. More laughs, they love his danger.

DANNY

You know in my cancellation exile I visited this tournament they have every year in one of the most racist parts of America. Seriously. I had to go in disguise so nobody tried to beat me up or ask me for an autograph.

Laughter.

DANNY

But really, this contest is held at a club for the richest, whitest, most racist motherfuckers on earth. It's been going on for years in Augusta, Georgia, and they don't even hide it. It's LITERALLY called . . . THE MASTERS.

The crowd explodes in laughs. He has them. Danny drags his cigarette, chuckling at his own joke.

OPENING TITLES: "THE TOURNAMENT"

INT. ARENA TUNNEL - MADISON SQUARE GARDEN - NIGHT

CORAL (twenties, dreadlocked, rap star, Juice WRLD type) swaggers off the arena stage into the dark tunnel. His impressive chain dances against his skin, glistening under each paparazzi camera flash.

Security and entourage flank Coral as the sold-out crowd in the arena chants his name, desperate for an encore. The arena quakes in the afterglow of Coral's inspired performance.

INT. GARAGE - MADISON SQUARE GARDEN - NIGHT

Coral makes his way with security through droves of crazy, drunk, and high, mostly white fans.

WHITE GIRL FAN

I want your babies, Coral!

TEENAGED WHITE BOY

You're better than Drake!

Coral waves but keeps moving toward his awaiting Sprinter Bus. A SEXY BRUNETTE (twenties) catches eye contact with Coral before he boards the bus. She makes pleading eyes. He looks away. She holds her gaze on him.

INT. SPRINTER BUS - MANHATTAN - NIGHT

Coral FaceTimes with his mom, MISS TINA (forties), as the Sprinter crawls in Saturday night NYC traffic. Coral slumps in his seat.

MISS TINA (ON FACETIME)

My pumpkin did an arena tour. Wow.

CORAL

Not done yet, Ma.

MISS TINA

One more night in the Big Apple. I *know* you in the streets tonight.

Coral sneaks two Percocets into his mouth and washes them down with a swig of lean while his mom looks away.

CORAL

I'd rather be back home for your birthday tomorrow. I'm tired, Ma.

MISS TINA

I've had forty-two birthdays. This is your first major tour. Enjoy what God's doing for you right now.

It's quiet for a beat.

MISS TINA

What is it, pumpkin?

CORAL

It's just weird, Ma. Twenty thousand white kids yelling . . .

QUICK FLASHBACK to Coral's show. He's onstage rapping as the crowd of mostly white teens yell along with him . . . *at* him.

CORAL ALONG WITH THE CROWD

NIGGAS DON'T KNOW I WAS TRAPPIN' AT THE TEXACO!!

QUICK CUT back to Coral in the Sprinter on FaceTime.

CORAL

Feels like I'm giving 'em permission.

MISS TINA

At least they're paying for it. And at least it's you on that stage. Not Jack Harlow or some shit.

They laugh.

CORAL

"Stages are cages." Kendrick said that.

MISS TINA

He did?

CORAL

Nah, but I knew you'd think that shit was wise if a OG said it.

MISS TINA

Boy bye. If Kendrick's a OG, what does that make me?

The WHITE DRIVER clocks Coral in the rearview.

INT. PENTHOUSE - LOWER EAST SIDE HOTEL - NIGHT - LATER

Coral's SECURITY GUARD lets him into the room. Coral gives him a dap, a nod, and continues talking to Miss Tina on FaceTime. The security guard disappears down the hall.

CORAL

Ma, look at this.

INT. PENTHOUSE - LOWER EAST SIDE HOTEL - NIGHT (CONTINUOUS)

Coral turns the phone to show her the ridiculous two-floor penthouse and its breathtaking view of Manhattan. While they're focused on the views SOMETHING darts behind Coral.

MISS TINA

God damn. The label pays for this?

Coral takes another swig of lean while she enjoys the view. WE HEAR something rattle in the room, but Coral misses it.

MISS TINA

Lemme see some more.

EXT. PENTHOUSE BALCONY - NIGHT - CONTINUOUS

Coral walks out to the balcony to give his mom a closer look. He leans over the edge of the balcony, wobbly from the drugs.

MISS TINA

Be careful. Hold it still. We don't have views like this in Bowie.

WE MOVE IN QUICKLY on Coral's back as he leans over the balcony rail. He LOSES HIS FOOTING but catches himself.

INT. PENTHOUSE - NIGHT

Coral walks up the stairs to the master bedroom. He's still holding the phone as Miss Tina chatters. He turns the corner and freezes. He SPOTS SOMETHING in the room.

The phone drops to the floor and Coral grips his gun in his jeans. He flicks on a light. It's RACHEL (SEXY BRUNETTE from the parking garage) sitting on the bed making sexy eyes.

MISS TINA (ON FACETIME)

You okay, C?

Coral shakes his head at Rachel. He picks up the phone so Miss Tina can't see what he sees.

CORAL

Ma, let me hit you back. Love you.

He hangs up the call and focuses back on Rachel.

CORAL

(with familiarity)

How? How do you do this?

INT. THE COMEDY CELLAR - MANHATTAN - NIGHT

Danny continues his stand-up. He owns the crowd.

DANNY

WHEEEEEEEEEEEEOOOOOOOOOO!

Danny makes wild eyes to go with the sound. The crowd erupts in laughter, some are in tears. Danny drags a cigarette.

DANNY

And look. I know most of y'all thought I was done. But you gotta be honest. I was onto something. Fifteen million trans women in the world . . .

The crowd hushes in anticipation.

ANGLE ON CLAIRE (thirties, white) who watches from the front row. Danny leans into the mic to make sure the crowd FEELS the punchline.

DANNY

Only one Rachel Dolezal in world history! That means a man is fifteen million times more likely to want to chop his dick off than a white person is to want to be Black!

The crowd bursts into laughter and naughty groans. Claire grins.

DANNY

Thank you all. You can't cancel me! I'm out! Thank you.

Danny steps off stage as the crowd stands and cheers.

INT. COMEDY CELLAR - BACKSTAGE AREA - NIGHT - MOMENTS LATER

HEATHER (forties, Black, Danny's wife) walks quickly through the hall just ahead of Danny.

DANNY

Baby, what are you doing?

Heather swings around. She's upset.

HEATHER

What are *you* doing? You said you were gonna take that last one out.

DANNY

I killed. Listen to them. They're buzzing.

HEATHER

You said you'd take it out.

DANNY

What are you, my manager now?

HUNTLEY (O.S.)

(South London accent)

That would be me.

HUNTLEY (forties, Black, suave) emerges backstage. He playfully punches and paws at Danny. Heather watches with disgust.

HUNTLEY

You. Were. PHENOMENAL. You're back, bruv, properly.

HEATHER

Huntley, did you have him put that last joke back in?

HUNTLEY

He's full grown, innit? He tells the jokes he wants.

Huntley turns his attention back to Danny.

HUNTLEY

Claire Shapiro from *Vanity Fair* is upstairs at the bar. She loved it. She wants to write a feature on you. One drink with her, bruv.

Danny looks to Heather.

DANNY

One drink, baby?

HUNTLEY

She's hoping for one with you, Danny. Just you. For the feature.

Danny pleads to Heather with a face.

HEATHER

You said you'd take Isaac to flag in the morning.

DANNY

I will, baby. One drink. One.

OFF Heather's relenting face.

INT. OLIVE TREE CAFE (ABOVE THE COMEDY CELLAR) - MANHATTAN

Huntley walks Danny into the trendy after-hours bar. They spot Claire at a table skimming her notes.

DANNY

I'm getting too old for this.

HUNTLEY

Allow it. This one's actually a writer.

DANNY

When did the writers get cleavage?

HUNTLEY

I'll be at the bar. Give you lot some space.

INT. BATHROOM - LONG ISLAND SUBURBAN HOUSE - NIGHT

ED (thirties, Black, square) rubs his hand over his clean-shaven face, staring in the mirror.

ED

My mom said this would happen.

Ed's wife, CHRISTINA (thirties, white), stands beside him checking out Ed's face in the mirror.

CHRISTINA

That you'd sell your company and be a millionaire? Of course she did. What better testament to her superior mothering?

ED

No, smart-ass.

Ed steps away from the mirror and pops Christina on the butt.

ED

She said if I married a white girl she'd make me shave my mustache.

CHRISTINA

And doesn't it look great?

Christina kisses Ed and stands beside him in the mirror.

CHRISTINA

I'm proud of you. And you dragged Jeremy along for the ride. You boys came a long way from Bowdoin water polo.

ED

He's my brother-in-law. And he brought the most important person in my life to me.

CHRISTINA

Aw, Ed . . .

ED

Our series A investor.

Christina playfully swats Ed. He bear hugs her. It's getting sexy then . . . a baby wails from outside the bathroom.

INT. BABY'S BEDROOM - LONG ISLAND HOUSE - MOMENTS LATER

Christina gently rocks CHLOE (infant) back to sleep. Ed is wearing a suit. Christina adjusts Ed's tie with one hand.

CHRISTINA

She'll grow up with a lot more than we did.

ED

Don't jinx it 'til the ink dries.

INT. UBER - BROOKLYN - NIGHT

Ed sits in the back, closes his eyes, and mutters a prayer. The WHITE DRIVER watches him in the rearview mirror.

INT. PETER LUGER STEAK HOUSE - BROOKLYN

Ed enters the old-fashioned steak house. He's surprised to find the restaurant empty except for

JEREMY (thirties, white, sweet-faced), TOM (sixties, white, stuffy), and CRAIG (sixties, white, looser). They're a few whiskeys in. Jeremy stands.

JEREMY

Eddy boy!

Ed puts on a shit-eating smile and embraces the three men. Tom and Craig stand and give Ed stiff handshakes. Jeremy gives Ed a rough, bro-y squeeze. They all sit.

JEREMY

Glad you came a little late, bud. I had time to get 'em lubed up. C.P. time, right?

The men chuckle. Ed laughs along reluctantly.

ED

You guys said eight. I'm ten minutes early.

JEREMY

Oh, shit. That's right, I forgot to tell you these guys moved it up.

TOM

It's fine. There must be loads of traffic coming from uptown around this time. Washington Heights?

ED

Long Island. I live in Glen Cove.

CRAIG

Fuck off, guys. Let's eat.

Craig waves over two servers carrying trays of food. Ed is reeling from the banter. Jeremy is oblivious.

INT. PRESS ROOM - BARCLAYS CENTER - NIGHT

LEBRANDON THOMAS (twenties, Black, tall, and muscular) sits beside his teammate WILL JAMISON (twenties, Black) during a somber press conference. Cameras flash on their cold, tired faces. Will's son WILLIE JR. (five) sits on his lap holding back a sad frown.

A REPORTER off-screen starts to ask *the* question.

REPORTER (O.S.)

LeBrandon, I've been covering you here in Brooklyn for six years. Three MVPs, five All-NBAs. You're the favorite son of this franchise. I know you've answered this question a hundred times, but now, after a third consecutive Finals loss, I have to ask . . .

Willie Jr. bursts into tears and looks up at LeBrandon.

WILLIE JR.

MY DADDY SAID YOU'RE MOVING TO CALIFORNIA, UNCLE L!

The room of reporters coos in sadness along with the little boy. LeBrandon cuts a glance at Will, who avoids eye contact. LeBrandon lifts sobbing Willie Jr. onto his lap for a hug.

INT. LOCKER ROOM - BARCLAYS CENTER - NIGHT

A QUICK MONTAGE. LeBrandon takes his last shower as a Brooklyn Nets player. LeBrandon gives "goodbye" daps and hugs to his teammates.

INT. LOCKER ROOM - BARCLAYS CENTER - NIGHT

LeBrandon is suited and alone in the locker room. He stares at his famous number 32 jersey hanging on his locker.

INT. OWNER'S SUITE - BARCLAYS CENTER - NIGHT

LeBrandon enters and finds Nets owner RALPH GIBSON (fifties, white, red-faced) sitting in his owner's suite. The suite overlooks the modern, empty arena with its sparkling wooden floors.

RALPH

Have a seat beside Ralphy, son.

LeBrandon does as he's told.

RALPH

I saw the presser.

LEBRANDON

I'm sorry, Mr. Gibson. You know I didn't want it to go that way.

RALPH

I know, L. That's never been how you handle yourself. You've been such a good kid since we got you from Kentucky. I'm grateful, son. You're leaving and I'm not here to try to talk you out of it.

LEBRANDON

You're not?

RALPH

C'mon, L. You know how I made my money, right?

LEBRANDON

Casinos, was it?

RALPH

You know how many poor idiots I've seen trick off their kid's college tuition at the blackjack table trying to chase their luck? We're both smarter than that. We've crapped out three years in a row here. I know you're out the door.

LeBrandon sighs in relief.

LEBRANDON

Wow. I've been dreading this conversation for three months. Thanks for making it easy on me.

RALPH

You said yourself a few years ago I'm like a father figure to you . . .

Ralph stands and walks to the bar and pours up two whiskeys.

RALPH

Well, a father knows his children. And while that beautiful body can do incredible things, things people have never seen before on a basketball court . . . It's your mind. Your mind is special, LeBrandon. You're gonna be the king of LA out there. On and off the court.

LEBRANDON

Thank you, Mr. Gibson. That means everything to me.

Ralph hands LeBrandon his drink. They clink glasses.

RALPH

Of course. But there is one more thing I wanna run by you.

INT. HOTEL BATHROOM - MANHATTAN - NIGHT

Coral and Rachel lay in the bathtub naked and high as fuck. Music wafts in from speakers. Coral slurs from the drugs.

CORAL

(laughing)

I don't even get it. You go from DC to Philly to New York three nights in a row. You got in my room, past security, three nights in a row.

RACHEL

You are soooo new to this. If you think *I'm* crazy, wait 'til you do your Europe tour.

They laugh. Rachel's phone rings outside the bathroom.

CORAL

Leave it.

RACHEL

It might be my mom.

CORAL

Wait. How old are you?

RACHEL

Seventeen.

Coral's face drops.

CORAL

I'm twenty-five. Give me a second.

She flicks him and steps out of the tub. Coral smiles.

INT. HOTEL BEDROOM - NIGHT - CONTINUOUS

Rachel, in a towel, grabs the phone from the dresser, peeking over her shoulder. The ringing coming from the phone is an alarm, not a phone call. Rachel places the phone back down beside Coral's pills and his gun. She stares at the gun.

INT. HOTEL BATHROOM - MANHATTAN - NIGHT - MOMENTS LATER

Coral looks up from the bath at Rachel's silhouette with sedated surprise.

CORAL

Yo! What are you doing?

ANGLE ON Rachel holding Coral's bottle of Percocets. She hangs the towel and slides her naked body back into the tub between Coral's legs. She pops open the bottle.

CORAL

No more. I'm not waking up with no OD'd white girl in here.

Teasingly, she holds a pill out of Coral's reach and sticks out her tongue as if she's going to down it. Coral swats the pill away. Rachel laughs and whispers.

RACHEL

I already took one.

She pulls from the bottle and drops a pill on Coral's tongue.

INT. OLIVE TREE CAFE (BAR ABOVE THE COMEDY CELLAR) - MANHATTAN - NIGHT

The bar has cleared besides Danny, Claire, the bartender, and Huntley, who sits at the bar out of earshot.

Danny and Claire are a few drinks in. They're comfortable and flirty. Claire jots notes into a pad as they talk.

CLAIRE

"Career Suicide." That's a bold tour name for someone, you know . . .

DANNY

Someone canceled?

CLAIRE

Don't flatter yourself. You weren't canceled. You just switched sides.

DANNY

Oh, I'm a sellout now?

CLAIRE

You know this little dance you do with white people.

DANNY

It's not a dance. It's S&M.
Don't write that down.

CLAIRE

Don't tell me how to do my job.

They share a sexy smile. Danny downs his drink. He raises his hand to signal to Huntley. Huntley brings two more drinks.

HUNTLEY

They're closing after you two finish these, so I'm gonna head. Claire, it's so lovely to meet you in person. Danny, in a bit.

DANNY

Aite bruh.

CLAIRE

So good to meet you.

Huntley leaves them alone in the empty bar. Danny and Claire clink glasses and drink. He's more drunk than she is.

DANNY

I don't switch sides. I don't have a side. I'm just a truth-teller.

CLAIRE

Okay then, truth or truth?

DANNY

Hmm. Truth.

CLAIRE

Okay. You know you killed downstairs. You know comedy has been suffering from withdrawal since you went on hiatus. And you know I had the feature thirty minutes ago.

Claire closes her notepad. She reaches over and thumbs at Danny's bracelet, twisting it slowly around his arm.

CLAIRE

So why are you still here with your fourth drink in your hand?

DANNY

Fifth. I had one onstage.

Danny rubs his hand against Claire's hand.

INT. PETER LUGER STEAK HOUSE BATHROOM - NIGHT

Ed stares at his face in the bathroom mirror. His eyes are red. He wipes a wet towel over his face and coughs. He shakes it all off and heads back into the restaurant.

INT. PETER LUGER STEAK HOUSE - NIGHT - MOMENTS LATER

Ed approaches the dinner table from behind. The restaurant remains empty. The men chat, not noticing Ed in earshot.

TOM

You were right about that one, Jeremy. Special.

JEREMY

(proud)

That's my guy.

CRAIG

Absolute unicorn.

Ed winces, not sure if he heard what he thought he heard. He shakes it off, walks into their line of vision, and sits down.

The men are pleasant. A small stack of papers rests on the table beside used dinner plates and cutlery.

CRAIG

Heyyy, how'd it go in there?

Ed clocks the papers.

ED

It was, uh . . . guys what's this?

TOM

We're so excited about having you and Jeremy and all of TechLabs join the East Water Holdings family, we just . . .

CRAIG

You sound so formal. Ed, man, we're just thrilled to buy TechLabs and get working with you guys, so we went ahead and put pen to paper.

JEREMY

Yeah bud. Why wait another day to be filthy fucking rich?

The men all laugh, Ed joins in. Ed coughs.

ED

Sorry. The beans. Spicy.

TOM

No worries. Yeah, the contract just needs your autograph.

Ed skims the documents. Ed reads down the page and stops on the big purchase number: $15 million.

ED

(Under his breath)

Jesus.

Ed coughs again. Ed sees Jeremy's signature and the signature line for Ed's name.

ED

(stalling)

Crazy that we're actually signing papers. I figured a DocuSign or . . .

CRAIG

Old money. Old-fashioned.

Ed starts to sign . . . then stops. He looks up at the men, who are all watching in eerily close anticipation.

JEREMY

Buddy? Buddy, sign the papers.

Ed coughs into his arm. He drops the pen.

ED

Craig, you said something a minute ago when I was walking back from the bathroom. What'd you call me?

CRAIG

Oh, I, I dunno. What do you mean?

ED

You called me a unicorn. What'd you mean by that?

TOM

Ah, he meant your company. You know, industry jargon. Special company you built. One of a kind.

ED

No, he wasn't. He was talking about me.

Jeremy stands up.

JEREMY

Uh. Bro. Can we talk?

ED

Nah. I'm not doing this.

CRAIG

Signing the papers is a formality. The deal is done.

Ed stands up from the table.

ED

Nothing's done until I sign.

Ed's eyes are bloodshot now. He tries to speak in between hard coughs as the men watch at the table.

ED

We'll find another buyer. They'll line up for us.
Jeremy, let's go . . .

Ed coughs uncontrollably. He hunches over to catch his breath. He's sweating, wobbling. He drops to the floor, knocking into the table. Jeremy rushes to him.

JEREMY

Holy shit, Eddy. Ed!

Ed whispers between gasps.

ED

I can't breathe. Get the pen. My Epipen. My jacket. Get it.

JEREMY

Get the Epipen from his jacket!

Tom rushes to hand Jeremy the syringe.

JEREMY

Stay here, bud! Stay with me!

Jeremy JAMS the syringe into Ed's thigh as he writhes on the floor. Ed's coughing subsides. His consciousness fades.

INT. DARK CORRIDOR - BARCLAYS CENTER - NIGHT

Ralph walks LeBrandon through the dark, empty corridors of the Barclays Center. Ralph's white SECURITY GUARD trails them out of earshot. LeBrandon towers over Ralph's stocky body.

RALPH

So here's what I'm thinking. Me and Mrs. Gibson are headed up to our estate in the Hamptons tomorrow for a few days. I know we can't change your mind, but we'll show you the best weekend of your life, kid . . .

LEBRANDON

I have appearances this weekend, and I should rest the knee . . .

RALPH

We'll take the chopper. Have some good scotch. Reminisce. You can hang on the beach, we'll invite some of your lady friends, maybe introduce you to some new ones.

LEBRANDON

The season just ended. I really need some time alone.

Ralph becomes more forceful.

RALPH

We've already prepared for your company, L. The chef brought that venison you like. We made up the guest house for you.

LeBrandon stops walking and faces Ralph.

LEBRANDON

No.

Ralph looks confused.

RALPH

What's that now?

LEBRANDON

I said no. I'm not going.

RALPH

We've already made the arrangements.

LEBRANDON

No. It's a complete sentence.

RALPH

You love our Hamptons place.

LEBRANDON

Mr. Gibson. Ralph. The players talk. I know this play. You and Mrs. Gibson take me up there. Get some weird photos of me doing coke in the pool or coming out of the shower or Mrs. Gibson hops in the bed with me and you two hold that shit over my head so I HAVE to re-sign here. You think I'm an idiot?

Ralph snorts a guilty, annoyed chuckle.

LEBRANDON

No. Thanks for the memories.

Ralph smiles.

RALPH

So smart. That's why we picked you.

Ralph taps twice on the door beside them. It SWINGS open and FOUR HULKING MEN run out and grab LeBrandon. The trailing security guard joins in. LeBrandon struggles with them, showing his strength and speed.

But the men are too much, punching and kicking him to the floor as Ralph watches, enjoying it. The security guard lands the knockout kick to LeBrandon's head and forces a syringe into his shoulder. LeBrandon's body goes limp.

INT. OLIVE TREE CAFE - MANHATTAN - NIGHT

We're in Danny's spinning POV staring at Claire, who is close, leaning in for a kiss. Just before she makes contact WE DROP to the floor, staring up at the swirling ceiling.

Claire stands overtop of us looking down, then walks out of frame. Our view of the bar ceiling shifts as Danny is dragged across the floor.

INT. HOTEL BATHROOM - MANHATTAN - NIGHT

Coral nods out of consciousness in the bathtub. Rachel watches in a towel beside the tub as the water drains around Coral. She's on the phone, her face concerned.

INT. CORRIDOR - NIGHT

Ralph watches his security team lift LeBrandon's unconscious body onto a stretcher.

INT. PETER LUGER STEAK HOUSE - NIGHT

Ed lies unconscious on the floor. Jeremy snaps his fingers in front of Ed's face twice to make sure he's out cold. Jeremy nods a confirmation to Craig and Tom. Craig munches on a string bean he's holding in his hand.

EXT. DOUBLE DECKER FERRY - UPPER DECK - THE NEXT DAY

A beautiful double-decker ferry glides over sparkling ocean under clear skies and sun. Ralph Gibson and his wife, BARBARA (fifties, white), hug while staring out over the blue sea toward an island in the distance. They're smiling, at peace.

Elsewhere on the deck Claire sunbathes, taking notes in a journal. Jeremy sits under an awning to avoid a sunburn.

Craig reads a newspaper with shades on while Tom feeds seagulls that fly alongside the boat.

Rachel sits alone, cross-legged with her head in her hands muttering to herself. She looks like she's going to be sick.

INT. MASTER BEDROOM - WESTCHESTER MANSION - DAY

Heather sits on a king-sized bed in a sprawling room with wide windows and cascading sunlight. She's dressed in weekend athleisure, calling Danny on the phone over and over.

Framed family photos of Heather, Danny, and their children, Isaac (eight) and Zoe (eighteen), adorn the walls. Danny's two Emmy awards and Heather's

NAACP Book Award stand prominently atop their large, wooden bookshelf.

Isaac plows into the room in his flag football uniform.

ISAAC

Where's Dad? We're gonna be late.

HEATHER

He's gonna meet us there. Go get your oranges out of the fridge.

ISAAC

Oranges? I wanted apple slices!

HEATHER

Isaac. Go. Now.

Isaac stomps out of the room.

EXT. FOOTBALL FIELD - RYE COUNTRY DAY SCHOOL - DAY

Preppy, pee-wee flag football teams face off. Isaac is among them wearing goofy rec-specs. Heather cheers him on from the packed bleachers, checking her phone between plays to see if Danny has responded.

The parents surrounding Heather in the bleachers are New York's bigwigs—mostly white, with a few other races sprinkled in. Heather stands out as a Black mom looking fly in her athleisure. JULIE (forties, visor, blonde ponytail) squeezes in beside Heather. Heather pretends to be happy to see her.

JULIE

Heather! Hiiiiii!

HEATHER

Hiiiii, Julieeeeeee!

JULIE

How are you?! OhmyGod. These boys from the city are rough. Right?

HEATHER

It's a rough game . . .

JULIE

(interrupting)

Where's Danny?

HEATHER

Uh, he's . . .

JULIE

(interrupting)

Girl. I saw a TikTok of him KILLING. IT. At the Comedy Cellar last night. I knew he'd be back on his feet. I told you.

HEATHER

I wouldn't say he was ever off his feet . . .

JULIE
(interrupting)
He's brilliant. And what he got "canceled" for was just so . . . Ugh. You wanna know what I think?

Julie hogs Heather's space and attention while the game carries on. Julie lowers her voice.

JULIE
Look. People should do whatever they want. It's a free country. Live how you want to live. But if Danny wants to think being trans is weird . . . not weird. Just funny. Funny! That's his job. He makes people laugh. He makes people happy. They can't take that from him. From us! Their whole trans thing is just funny. That's all he was trying to say.

HEATHER
It was?

JULIE
I mean, you would know. He's your husband. What do I know? What do you think?

HEATHER
Well . . .

JULIE
(interrupting)
My master's philosophy class is reading Danny's book this semester. They're

obsessed. I feel like such a schmuck
doing this. But a few students asked for
autographs. I didn't want to promise, but
if it's not too much. For the kids . . .

HEATHER

I can sign 'em. We did co-write the book.

Julie is visibly less excited about Heather signing the books, but she tries to hold face.

JULIE

Oh. Yeah. They'd love that. I have
a young lady from the East Bronx—
Veronica. She adores you.

Isaac scores a touchdown and the parents cheer. Heather and Julie join in. Isaac looks to the sideline searching for his parents.

His face drops when he clocks that Danny is still absent. Heather holds a supportive smile. The cheers die down and Julie starts right back into her spiel.

JULIE

What was I saying? Danny! Wait is he
here? It's almost halftime. But I'm sure
he had *a night* with the show and all.

HEATHER

He's not feeling great.

JULIE

Oh no! Wait. Heather. I know you, sis.

What's that voice? Oh my God. Is it the drinking again? He must be so anxious going back onstage.

HEATHER

Can you keep your voice down? I didn't say that.

Julie holds Heather's hand tenderly.

JULIE

I'm here for you and your family, sis. Whatever it is. That man has a voice this world needs to hear. We are your community and we will stand by him while he gets back up on that horse.

Julie pulls Heather into an unwelcome hug. Heather is drowning. She stares ahead at the field with a fake smile.

CUT TO: DARKNESS.

Over Black WE HEAR a robotic voice repeat:

"Incomplete Roster. Start Time Delayed." Every fifteen seconds, it repeats: "Incomplete Roster. Start Time Delayed."

INT. THE PIT - DAY

WE are in Ed's POV as he pushes himself out of a sensory deprivation tank. Sunlight pours in and blinds him for a moment. He looks down and clocks that he's in his underwear.

WE STAY in Ed's POV as his vision clears and we see he is in a giant, empty pit carved out below ground level like the World Trade Center Monument. The sides are twenty feet high, opening straight up to the sky. The walls are made of slick, reflective, black metal.

Ed rubs his eyes, searching for the source of the robotic voice, but before he can find it, he clocks three Black figures in underwear, faces painted like black-and-white skull candy masks.

Three more sensory deprivation chambers sit in each corner of the cube.

Ed panics and scurries for a place to hide from the three other figures, but there's nowhere.
WE SEE that the figures are Danny, Coral, and LeBrandon. LeBrandon and Coral are approaching. Danny watches.

ED

Get the fuck away from me! Back up!

CORAL

Bro, chill. Chill!

ED

What is this? Who are you?

LEBRANDON

We could ask you the same question.

Ed recognizes the voice coming from the tall figure.

ED

LeBrandon Thomas?

LEBRANDON

How the fuck do you know my name? You got something to do with this?

DANNY

They know your name on Mars, nigga.

ED

Danny Watts?

DANNY

And that's our son, Lil' Yachty.

CORAL

Okay. Jokes.

ED

Where are we? What's this makeup?

LEBRANDON

We been trying to figure that out for . . . I don't know. A long time.

CORAL

No phones. No watches.

DANNY

No keys, no wallets. And no Goddamn cigarettes. Shit.

Danny walks over to a stainless steel cube that looks like a shiny toolbox in the center of the pit. The voice is coming from the cube.

"Incomplete Roster. Start Time Delayed."

Danny kicks the cube. It doesn't budge.

DANNY

I think she got the answers.

CORAL

We all woke up in those lil' spaceship things.

ED

Okay, let's think about this logically. Where did you guys each fall asleep last night?

DANNY

Who made you Leonardo? We already had this conversation.

LEBRANDON

Yeah. What's your story?

ED

I was at dinner with my business partner. And these two old-money private equity guys. We were about to sell our company, but I think there must have been peanut oil in the food, 'cus I . . . I . . .

DANNY

Okay, you're a really boring storyteller.

CORAL

Let him finish.

DANNY

Fuck that. It's getting dark.

LeBrandon pushes on the walls, looking for an escape.

ED

LeBrandon, hoist me up on your shoulders. I'll pull myself out and find help.

LEBRANDON

How do I know you'll come back?

CORAL

You don't even know where we are.

DANNY

You could stand on two LeBrandons, you ain't getting over that wall, big boy.

The men bicker as the sun sets above them in the pit.

INT. THE PIT - NIGHT (LATER)

It's dark now except for the glow from the sensory deprivation tanks. The guys wait around hopelessly. The computerized voice drones: "Incomplete Roster.

Start Time Delayed." Ed tries a few last pathetic calls for help.

ED

Help! Can somebody hear me?!

Coral lies on his side. He's starting to sweat from Percocet withdrawal. Danny searches around inside his tank.

DANNY

They can keep my shit, I just want my cigarettes.

LeBrandon sits cross-legged, meditating. Danny clocks him.

DANNY

Allah can't hear us down here.

CORAL

You know a better way?
Or you just gonna keep talking?

DANNY

The latter, unless you got a ladder.

CORAL

I'm tired of hearing your voice.

DANNY

Then cover your ears, Buckwheat.

They're getting testy.

ED

Guys, please. Let's keep cool.

DANNY

You shut your corny ass up.

Coral starts toward Danny. They're about to clash when—SHOOSH!

A blinding white floodlight fills the cube. The four men freeze, squinting in the light.

They look up to the edge of the cube to where the giant floodlight stands behind eight silhouettes, too dark to make out. All four men yell up at the silhouettes. "HELP! HELP US! GET US OUT OF HERE!"

One of the silhouettes steps forward. Danny recognizes him.

DANNY

Huntley!? Yo, get me out of here!

HUNTLEY

I'm afraid I can't just yet, Danny.

DANNY

What? C'mon, let's go.

Huntley shakes his head.

DANNY

The fuck are you doing? Get me up. Heather's probably flipping out.

HUNTLEY

(matter-of-factly)

It's the tournament, innit?

The men in the pit look at each other in confusion.

DANNY

Huh?

Huntley looks to the other silhouettes. One of the silhouettes whispers to Huntley. Huntley continues as if he is reading from instructions.

HUNTLEY

(to the men in the pit)

Yeah, bruv. You lot are a team. The Unicorns. But eventually there'll be just one of you. The winner. He'll go home and his sponsors will get the prize.

Danny chuckles.

DANNY

Okay, Huntley, you got me. Heather, kids, y'all can come out now! My birthday isn't for two weeks. Y'all get crazier every year with this shit, I swear.

Huntley doesn't budge.

DANNY

C'mon. It's getting cold down here.

Ed steps forward and yells up at Huntley.

ED

You said sponsors. What kind of sponsors?

HUNTLEY

Well, me and Claire here are Danny's sponsors. You each have your own.

Claire steps forward in the light so Danny can see her. She's smiling slightly.

Coral makes out Rachel's face beside Claire. Rachel looks guilty. She mouths: "Sorry." The men are confused.

HUNTLEY

(ashamed)

Danny, I'm gutted to do this to you mate. You know the strain I'm in with the IRS. My kids. I was really counting on my commissions from your tour before you tanked yourself. But the pot of this thing is massive. I'll break you off something if you win, bruv.

DANNY

(losing patience)

Huntley, what are you saying? Get me out of here right now.

HUNTLEY

I can't do that. Not yet, anyway. I'm sorry.

Ralph Gibson steps forward. LeBrandon's eyes widen.

RALPH

You got the gist, L? Just beat out these punks and you go back to your life, kid. You're stronger. You're smarter. Piece of cake.

LEBRANDON

(in disbelief)

Ralph? Is this about me re-signing? I mean, we can revisit with my agent. But this isn't gonna help.

RALPH

(ignoring LeBrandon)

All right! Everybody knows the game. Let's get this party started.

Ralph Gibson SHOVES HIS FOOT in Huntley's back sending him flying into the pit. Huntley scrambles to his feet and yells up at the sponsors.

HUNTLEY

(enraged)

Hey! This is not what we discussed! You . . .

The cube lets out a piercing BEEEEEEEEP, cutting off Huntley's rage. The men in the pit grimace and cover their ears. The beep ends and the cube speaks.

THE CUBE

Five Unicorns. Roster complete. Round One is called: One Round. You have sixty seconds to reduce the roster to Four Unicorns or all participants will be eliminated.

The cube beeps again and opens, revealing a 9mm pistol inside. Huntley bolts for it while the others are in shock.

THE CUBE

Fifty-nine, fifty-eight, fifty-seven . . .

Danny, LeBrandon, and Coral chase, but Ed is shell-shocked. The sponsors cheer them on from up above.

THE SPONSORS

Go LEBRANDON! C'mon, Coral! Yeah, Danny! Get in there, Ed!

Huntley grabs the gun first and points it at the others one by one to back them off. The sponsors hush.

Huntley grips the gun with both hands and looks up at the sponsors, who back away from the edge of the cube for safety. They watch from the shadows.

THE CUBE

Forty-nine, forty-eight . . .

Huntley yells up to the sponsors.

HUNTLEY

You fucking lying cunts!

LeBrandon tries to sneak-attack Huntley, but Huntley aims the gun back at him, freezing him.

Huntley points the gun at each of the men in the pit. His eyes go wild.

ED

Listen, please. It's not real. Think about it. This is crazy.

HUNTLEY

It's BLOODY REAL! They're mental! They've got twisted shit lined up. Sick shit. They're gonna make us WISH we were eliminated.

THE CUBE

Thirty-five, thirty-four . . .

DANNY

You fucking sellout.

Huntley points the gun at Danny.

HUNTLEY

That's enough, mate! No more.

ED

STOP! Listen to me! IT'S NOT REAL. IT'S NOT LOGICAL. WHY US?

HUNTLEY

You're the bloody favorites! You're chosen!

Huntley aims at Danny and prepares to pull the trigger, then . . .

DANNY

WAIT! Do the kid.

Huntley looks at Coral, whose face curls up in fear.

DANNY

He's the smallest. He's the weakest. He's the dumbest.

Huntley aims the gun at Coral, then Danny. Back to Coral.

DANNY

You said we're a team at first. Look at him, he's already sweating. He'll be deadweight.

THE CUBE

Twenty-six, twenty-five . . .

DANNY

C'mon, Hunt. Think! Look at him. He's useless.

ED

Put it down. It's not real. It can't be real.

Huntley wipes tears from his eyes. He takes deep breaths. He listens to Ed and starts to lower the gun, but then, BANG!

A gun fires in the distance. The men jump in surprise.

Huntley raises the gun to point straight at Danny's head.

HUNTLEY

Sorry, mate.

Huntley pulls the trigger. BANG! LeBrandon, Coral, and Ed recoil. As they open their eyes they see . . .

Huntley's body drops to the ground, his head a splattered mess of bloody brains, bone, and tissue. The gun exploded in Huntley's face.

The remaining four Unicorns approach and look down at Huntley's limp body and demolished face in horror.

THE CUBE
(cheerfully)
Unicorn eliminated. Four Unicorns advance. Congratulations.

The watching sponsors up above applaud lightly in satisfaction. They sound like a polite crowd at a tennis match.

Rachel clenches her teeth, frustrated to see one of her Unicorns eliminated from competition.

BANG! Another gun fires in the distance, followed by polite applause.

WE PULL OUT way up above the pit, revealing a dozen more pits on the island, each with four Black contestants in face paint down below and sponsors watching from the edges. Here and there an excited sponsor lets out a "Yeah!"

BANG! Another gunshot lights up the sky. WE HEAR the thud of a body drop and more polite Sponsor applause.

CUT TO BLACK: BANG!

TITLES OVER BLACK: THE TOURNAMENT

MUSIC CUE: "The Whole World" by Outkast

END OF EPISODE.

5

Expats and Allies

Of course, not all attacks on Blackness are as violent and final as a gunshot. Some attacks are more subtle and needling. Some burn slowly.

By my late twenties, I had left Google and started to look for new ways to define myself and make money. I got the idea to define myself by *how* I made money. I attached myself to the identity of entrepreneur. It was the sexiest and most nebulous moniker among twenty- and thirtysomething techie types who were just floating from job to job, trying to find the best combination of equity and work-life flexibility to get rich quick while never having to feel like we were actually working. I had lived in London for a brief stint while working at Google, and then I had a run in Berlin, where I tried and failed to launch a new location for the tech startup that employed me after I quit. The tech industry was starting to lose its shine a bit, but I was nonetheless in love with this idea of myself as wandering *entrepreneur*, someone who danced around the globe partying and endearing myself to clients and investors, trying to alchemize a fortune for me and whoever would back my escapades.

I didn't invent that lifestyle. There were, and still are, hordes of American-born in-between-jobbers presenting themselves as *thought leaders*, or *creatives*, or, naturally, *entrepreneurs* popping around all over the globe. They travel in packs, showing up to gobs of invite-only, for-profit conferences like Summit at Sea. They migrate to Nevada yearly for Burning Man, pretending to be bohemian and interesting, when in reality they are just the adult children of wealthy people seeking meaning and a feeling of community among other wealthy children of wealthy people. And, of course, as a pack, they are extremely white. Even with small freckles of people of color mixed into their swarm, and despite their best efforts to appear liberal and worldly, their culture is, even at its best, at least slightly anti-Black.

It occurred to me while trying to define myself as an entrepreneur that I should become a part of this community. I thought, correctly, that doing so would create opportunities for me that would lead to money. I also thought that people who led with their liberal leanings and wore printed scarfs and funky hats would accept me—a Black person—in a way that the cargo shorts and hoodies hadn't been able to. Furthermore, during my time in London and Berlin, I fell for the fable that anti-Black racism lives only in the US and that somehow when you fly across the ocean it magically dissipates. It's more fun to believe that. It makes the rest of the world seem like some shimmering pool of safe haven that might offer us refuge if we can just afford to get there. *There* being anywhere but *here*. (Never mind that time when the white guy standing in line outside my favorite Berlin bar spotted me and complained to the bouncer, "Yieu let een da Colored mehn inshted aff meeee?")

In 2016, I went on a trip to Israel with a group of forty social entrepreneurs under the age of forty, most of whom boasted full membership in this amorphous pack of jobless vagrants with self-aggrandizing LinkedIn titles. I wasn't a social entrepreneur—nor have I ever been such a thing—but I was working at a tech startup where we taught aspiring career changers how to code with a stated ambition to improve racial and gender representation in the tech industry. In reality, the company actually made the industry whiter, as its program's outrageous cost priced out most people of color. Most of the students who paid thousands of dollars to take our nineteen-week coding boot camp looked like the rest of the industry: white guys in shorts and thong sandals. And yet, because of the company's *stated* mission—to help diversify Silicon Valley—I was able to squeeze myself into the application's "social entrepreneur" category.

The application also required that I explain my interest in Israel. I wrote something about growing up in Montgomery County, Maryland, in schools with high populations of Jewish students. I wrote that I was interested to learn how Jewish people had elevated from atrocities in ways that I could apply to the Black community. I was pandering, a bit. I've noticed that people become generous when I make myself small and doughy eyed and appeal to their wisdom. *O teach me your ways, you wise and brave soul.*

I was also required to submit a short video so that they could get a feel for me as a person. I used my phone to take a selfie video in my tiny Brooklyn studio apartment. I was charismatic and smiley and dorky in the video. I remember thinking that this was my chance to show them that I was, in fact, Black; if there was some racial quota to be met, I thought, maybe this video would help me. I knew from my time in the tech industry that combining my Blackness with a friendly and curious affect formed an impression that could get me into certain doors.

The video and application worked, and I was chosen to attend the trip. And I'm glad, because that trip exposed me to a beautiful and dangerous and tense part of the world that most people are only able to read about in the news and in holy texts.

The Schusterman Family Foundation took the forty of us there as a part of their Reality Global program, which is meant to expose impactful people to Israel and one another as a means of philanthropy and networking. I was in my mid-twenties. We hopped from Jerusalem to Tel Aviv to Nazareth indulging in fantastic meals and wine—so much wine—and sleeping in nice hotels and lying on beautiful beaches. All of this was paid for by the foundation minus the $700 airfare.

And there were a few on the trip who were older than I was, who had seen and read more about the world—and certainly Israel—who whispered that the *real* intent of the trip was propaganda. They said we'd been brought here to be taught a specific version of the history of Israel, one that portrayed it as righteous in its conflict with Palestine. But I was so taken by the extravagance and beauty that I never dug any deeper, even as we traipsed to the border of Syria and stepped into the shells of buildings that had been annihilated by bombs and weaponry. I was on this trip to explore and meet people and drink wine, and I didn't bother to interrogate beyond what was offered to me by our experiential guides. I regret that.

But this was an otherwise phenomenal trip for me, and it spawned the career and identity reset I had been wanting since leaving my corporate job at Google a few years prior. I felt free in another country, wading through the mud in the Dead Sea and talking over hummus and espressos with these do-gooders. I was, of course, out of my element, but finding myself disoriented in a new place is a form of freedom I've always cherished. In my early twenties I fell in love with the sensory overload I felt living in Berlin for a short time—alone, unsettled, and living in a very different time zone than most of the people I knew. But I wasn't *actually* alone here in Israel. I was surrounded by ex-pats like me, but with my guard down because we weren't in America. I had to be vulnerable to let in these new surroundings and experiences.

Each night in Israel was a small rager, as we all poured out into the bars in Tel Aviv, Haifa, Jerusalem, you name it. The social marathon was so intense that one morning I vomited in the bathroom in the Holocaust Museum. (I'm not proud of that, but it's the truth, and evidence of how hard we were partying that week.) I needed a break, so that night I decided to hang back with a small crew that was chatting in the hotel lobby.

Of the handful of folks present for this conversation, I only remember two: There was Eliza, a tall, white woman from Oakland. A few years older than me, with kind eyes, she tried to make me feel comfortable around all these white people in a way that didn't end up making me feel even more uncomfortable, which is a rare and adept form of actual allyship. I could never prove that she was intentionally trying to make me feel more comfortable, but I knew it, and I appreciated her eye contact, smiles, and attention when I had something to say. Eliza was slouching on a lobby couch, her eyes hanging heavy in that delirious, giggly fog people go into when they should really be in bed but the bed is too far.

And then there was Ira. Ira was a short white guy with a quick, sharp wit. Ira was a fake ally. His "allyship" was expressed with provocative, long-winded mini-speeches delivered to groups of people. It was pure performance, intended only to capture more audience and to prove himself the most eloquent, well-meaning white guy in the room—or maybe even the world. He would say things like, "We could solve a lot of problems in this country if everyone could understand that Black people are just like white people . . . they're just Black," with a pregnant pause for comedic timing. Some would chuckle, some would give a thoughtful snort, and I would grimace behind a smile. But until this conversation, Ira had me fooled. I thought he was "well-intentioned," if a little too in love with the sound of his own voice. (And to be fair, he was funny as hell in moments).

As we all started to drift into sleepiness in the lobby, he spotted a moment to catch us off guard with a joke he'd been crafting and perhaps trying on other audiences. He sat upright and leaped into his bit.

"You know what the best thing is about being a white guy?" he asked.

I was paralyzed immediately. When white people start talking about being white, I know I'm about to be sideswiped, but I never know exactly how. So I freeze and tense my joints, bracing as if I were in a car stalling out in a busy intersection—certain that I'm about to suffer a collision but unsure of where the blow will come from. I noticed Eliza sink into her seat. She noticed me noticing her, but she knew there was nothing she could do to save me. Ira was building momentum, and she didn't want to be a meat shield for me in the face of his "biting" humor.

Ira continued: "I can walk into any Four Seasons in the world and take a shit and nobody will stop me."

He puffed out his chest, looked down, and laughed at his own joke until he turned red. The other white people sitting with us guffawed. Eliza sunk deeper and avoided eye contact with me.

"Ira . . . ," she said. She sort of shook her head. I felt like I needed to respond. I felt like I needed to say or do something. All I did was grin (no teeth) and perform an exaggerated, fake sigh. I was trying to show the rest of them that I was in on the joke even while being the butt of the joke.

"Hardy-har! That's so true! You can take a shit wherever you want because you're white, Ira! But we're still both people, ain't we? Sitting here enjoying a laugh together. Global racism ain't so bad. Hardy-hardy-har."

I felt smacked in the face because what he said was true and tested, presumably. And here I was sitting in the lobby of a very nice hotel with a group of white people who were now suddenly being made aware that I hadn't been stopped by hotel security on the way in perhaps *because* I was with Ira and the rest of them. I thought about punching Ira. Or dragging him by his polo onto the floor. But I couldn't move, much less attack. This is honesty.

I thought about Ira's joke for the remaining days of that trip and for years after. I think about it each time I walk into a bar in Williamsburg or Ridgewood during the heavy hours and notice the bartenders and a few patrons giving me extra, unwanted attention. I think about it when I walk into the Hungry Ghost coffee shop in Park Slope, right across the street from the studio where I record my podcasts, and notice the white folks noticing me. I think about it when I stumble into a restaurant on the white side of Bushwick and ask to use the bathroom. In each of these places I consider what Ira said while I straighten my posture and fix my tone to seem as unthreatening as possible to the white staff. I assume, because he told me as much, that if I looked like Ira, I could live through those moments without a second thought. I could be weightless and unaware. I could just drift in and out of any establishment and take a shit wherever I pleased. According to Ira, that's a defining trait of whiteness.

In two sentences, in that lobby, Ira took me out of the freedom I was so enjoying halfway across the globe. I've learned from comedians that a joke works when its punchline is surprising and inevitable. Ira was right. He had access to all the world's most beautiful and convenient amenities by way of being white. And he wielded that truth to feel powerful and clever at my expense just before bed. He probably slept like a baby that night.

I still think about Ira in that lobby. Taking his glasses off to wipe his moist, red face as he coughed out his last few chuckles at his joke. Peeking at me to see how I was stomaching my embarrassment.

He knew he hurt me. He wanted to hurt me. Because that meant his joke landed.

I hope I see him again.

6

Encounter with a Geniuth

I quit my job at Google in 2014 because the dehumanization I felt in the building outweighed the confidence boost offered by the prestige of being a Google employee. After three years and change, I was bored and exhausted by the cycle of hustling to look like I was working hard and making an impact at the end of each quarter. I had entered the company with dreams of someday running the entire place. It sounds ridiculous to admit it now. But I was young and naïve and lacking in self-awareness. Companies like Google make a point of inflating the dreams and egos of their young new hires like me so that they'll work extra-long hours and make sacrifices for the gains of an employer who will never love them back nor repay them equitably. It took me a couple years to realize that I wasn't a star performer by any metric at Google and that I was going to struggle to build relationships with higher-level executives at the company who could help pull me up because I wasn't native to Silicon Valley culture, Ivy

League culture, and most importantly, white culture. I had to face the truth that the company was telling me I was mediocre. And that made me, someone searching for esteem by way of bonuses and accolades, severely uncomfortable.

I remember preparing a quitting spiel to give to my manager at the time, who I expected to feel undermined and abandoned by my leaving seemingly out of nowhere. I teared up in our last one-on-one, which took place in a sterile, bland conference room, preparing to deliver the blow. When I finally said the words—*I'm leaving*—I watched my manager's mouth turn up into a soft, sympathetic smile. She cried. She was happy for me, she said. She was proud to see me taking control of my career and my life. She acknowledged that I was always going to be Little Brother at Google. I packed up my cubicle, and by the end of the following week my ID card that got me through security was deactivated.

I had left the mothership. I was out in the wild. But not really. I had already landed a job at the tech startup where I'd later meet Brett and Owen, the guys who taught me how to monetize my victimhood. I was too afraid of life after Google to leave without new employment, and I was living check to check in Manhattan, so I made sure the ink was dry on my new employment contract before I said goodbye to my Google boss with puffy, red eyes.

I felt untethered without the religion of Google in my life, but I also felt more like an adult. I was still insecure and very much looking to money and job titles for validation, but I felt more like myself now, on the hunt for opportunities that served me instead of hiding behind those six big colorful letters.

In the summer of 2014, shortly after leaving Google, I went to a party in one of those three-story Williamsburg lofts that make you wonder how anyone young enough to throw a party could possibly afford this much square footage in gentri-Brooklyn. It was glamorous to have a job at a tech startup at that time—I thought so, at least—and I felt I had outkicked my coverage by getting a head of sales role at one that paid $90K a year.

My coworkers and I went out to parties often after work back then. The tech startup scene consisted of a ton of kids in their mid to late twenties making much more money than I was, so the parties could be pretty extravagant. Sometimes there were ice sculptures or piles of mushroom candies available upon entry. There were DJs and sometimes even live performers. I heard Thundercat's music for the first time when I saw him performing live for about forty tech startup heads rolling on Molly. The money. The whiteness. The energy of New York nightlife. Together it all created this flicker of what felt like freedom that I could feel on my skin. But it didn't really pass through me the way it looked like it did for these white kids swaying their bodies around aimlessly like the wax inside lava lamps as if there were no music playing at all.

At some point, I made my way up to the roof to get some air. Black folks like me do a large amount of going outside to get some air at white parties. There was just one other person up there, a gangly twentysomething, roughly my age (twenty-six), smoking a cigarette by himself and looking out across the East River toward the Manhattan skyline. He was wearing a striped polo that drooped over his boney shoulders. He had a pale, boyish face, but sort of carried himself like he had some wisdom. He had a lisp.

He offered me a cigarette, which I passed if my mom's reading this.

I started to make small talk. Back then, when I met a new white person, I always tried to talk first so I could direct the conversation somewhere that wouldn't make me squeamish. I still do that in certain situations.

He cut me off before I could waste both of our time. He asked me what I did for a living. With much gusto, I told him about my sales job at the tech startup that was surely going to "change the world" (and which has since gone defunct). He listened to a few more sentences of my yakety-yak before taking over. I'm not sure he even heard what I said. It just felt like a timer went off in his head signaling that my turn was finished and now the floor was his for as long as he decided.

And I accepted.

He began spieling me by telling me about the company *he* worked for. His body inflated and he rolled his head back on his shoulders, looking up at the sky as he prophesied that the company would change how people did *something*—I can't remember what—forever. He revealed that it was *his* company, that he had raised millions of dollars, and sold some of his shares while holding on to majority ownership so he could be *comfortable* while he built this darling business that was going to have such an impact. He revealed that we were sitting on *his* rooftop, and that all three of the floors beneath us belonged to him. He told me that he sometimes came up to the rooftop even with guests in his house to have visions about how his company would grow before he went back down to entertain.

He was certain that the plan would play out just as he expected. I was knocked over by his confidence. At that age I wasn't yet cynical about mid-twenties bravado. I asked him, earnestly, how he knew everything he said was going to happen.

He really looked at me for the first time right in my eyes. He answered with a clarity and surefootedness as if I'd asked how old he was.

"Because I'm a Goddamn geniuth," he said with his lisp. He believed that shit.

This specific creature fills most jobs that pay anywhere from a couple hundred thousand dollars a year up into the highest ranks of C-suite millionaires. He is roughly 5'10" with a white, stubbled face and semi-neat haircut that he tends to once every four or five weeks. He speaks in long-winded stories and with a tonal authority that makes it sound like he's reading from a Wikipedia page. He is energized by the sound of his own voice and the rise he gets from holding you there, nodding and smiling under the weight of his filibustering as he plows through each anecdote and punchline, leaving just enough space for you to give him nonverbal affirmation, but not enough for you yourself to speak.

He is between the ages of twenty-five and fifty-five, but he stopped evolving emotionally at twenty-five. He wears fitted jeans and a Patagonia vest if he's in tech or finance. He wears a light-colored cotton Henley with shades on his forehead if he works in entertainment. He is not cool, but you say he is to your friends, who know that you mean he is a manageable enough hang for a white guy, but that you wouldn't hang with him at all if you didn't work together. And, naturally, he is your boss.

He's the head of product at a tech startup. He's the VP of scripted television at a production company. He's the youngest provost in school history at a university where his uncle is the president. He's a partner at a private equity firm or consulting company. And he is certain that he's overqualified even for the $450K/year role that he's in, despite being promoted into that role by a four-years-older mentor version of himself and despite being less qualified, less creative, and taking more vacations than the women and people of color who report to him.

No. He's certain that this high-paying job is just a pit stop on the way to his destiny. His heroes are Elon Musk and Steven Spielberg and Steve Kerr, though he may not say so out loud if he lives in a coastal city. But he looks at them and sees himself.

White. Smug. Capitalizing. Male. Boyish. Unaged and unweighted by taking care of others or working for anyone's dreams or well-being but his own. Impressed by his own boldness to wear Jordans with a suit.

I've known this creature in his many forms. After all, I used to work in Silicon Valley, and I now work in entertainment. His freedom to live exactly as he pleases is only fettered by the distress it causes him that he hasn't bypassed *more* people on the company org chart; by the fact that his roommate from Dartmouth manages twice as many people at a competing company and owns a house twice as big as his on the quiet side of the Jersey Shore. In other words, his freedom is only restricted in his mind by comparing himself to another, richer white guy who seems more free.

Sometimes I think the same applies to me and other Black folks. Sometimes I think that enslavement lives only in the mind. I think that if we stopped comparing ourselves to the freedoms other people seem to have, we'd then be free ourselves. I think that if we just behaved as if we were free, then it would be so. Millennial Insta-philosophers offer that gratefulness and abundance thinking are keys to happiness. In tweets and well-edited TikTok videos they implore us to focus on what we *do* have, not what we are lacking. They insist that those of us seeking mental freedom and the joy that comes with it should only accept that we already have what we want. But as someone sensitive to every force that impinges my freedom, I recognize those Insta-philosophers as yet another force pushing its point of view into my mind as I scroll, restricting my own thoughts, reminding me that I'm not yet free.

I'm not yet as free as the lispy tech CEO who could be accepted by venture capitalists and investors as a genius just by proclaiming he was one. I'm not yet as free as those venture capitalists themselves, who have the resources to propel that young tech CEO toward shaping the world as he, and his investors, want to see it shaped: in their image. I've just recounted two different types of freedom—to self-define, and to mandate—and there are many other forms of freedom that I value. I value freedom of time, to stand atop a beautiful three-story loft in New York City and meditate while your guests inside enjoy your space. I value the freedom that such a space offers. So many of my own discomforts living in New York can be reduced to the lack of space and time.

I want the freedom to try and fail. When I scan the Wikipedia pages and IMDBs of modern titans of industry like Elon Musk in tech or Ari Aster in film, I find near the bottom of the page a graveyard of projects and experiments that didn't succeed. Eventually, after many failures, those people find success, and they're celebrated for the wins while the losses are pushed to the margins of the page. But can I follow that formula? Several years ago, I shot a short film using money out of my own pocket, along with some cash borrowed from friends and my producer. Just as we began our plan to screen the film around the country, Covid struck. After our New York and Atlanta screenings, we shut down touring the film, and I haven't had the time or energy to resuscitate it in the years since. That's $80K down the drain for me and the other producers. I plan to take another shot at directing, and I'll have to borrow more money from whoever will get behind my vision. But I know I'm in a rare seat to even be able to ask friends for money for such a venture. Most Black people don't have such access. That's a restriction on our freedom of imagination. It hurts to envision things that you don't have the resources to build.

I'm reminded of Kanye West, who seems like someone seeking freedom. He, in particular, seems to feel trapped by the ways other people see him because he is Black. I imagine he wishes people would accept him as a genius the way the lisped genius accepted himself. Kanye proclaims himself a genius. He seems like he has anchored his ideas of freedom and genius to some form of male whiteness. If you watch Kanye West's famous interviews on *The Breakfast Club* or *Sway in the Morning*, you'll hear Kanye complain that people try to hold him back and put him down by labeling him a rapper and comparing him to other Black artists, when they should really be comparing him to people like Steve Jobs and Walt Disney. I take it that Kanye believes there's a level at the top—the white boy genius level—that he should have reached in the minds of audiences, but that he can't reach it because he's held back by Blackness. When he struggled to find financing for his Yeezy shoes and clothing line a few years ago, Kanye exclaimed into microphones that he needed his version of the Medici family to patronize him the way the Medicis patronized famous white boy artists like Michelangelo, Raphael, Donatello, and Leonardo da Vinci.

Kanye's not the first, though he may have been the loudest, to want the sort of creative freedom afforded to white boys. There have been countless studies and stories in recent years about the disparity between funding offered to white founders across industries vs. the funding and investments offered to people of color. So many Black entrepreneurs and creatives envy that freedom to create, that freedom to try and fail on someone else's dime.

But what pisses me off on a more human level isn't just how that disparity in funding widens the opportunity gap. What really makes me mad is that it makes white boys think they somehow deserve those opportunities. For every twenty-five Mark Zuckerberg clones who fail and tank their ideas and investment cushions, there is one who succeeds and finds his face on the front page of the *Wall Street Journal* and in headlines that whip around the *Hollywood Reporter* or *TechCrunch* magazine. And his success emboldens swaths of more stubbly faced pseudo entrepreneurs to label themselves geniuthes, slap together pitch decks, and raise money toward new fail machines. Meanwhile there are thousands of would-be Black creators watching along, wanting to take the same risks, but feeling hamstrung by lacking resources or facing imposter syndrome because the faces on the magazines behind the Billion-Dollar Companies never look like theirs.

7

Blinding Lights

"Chaos is a ladder."

—LORD BAELISH, *GAME OF THRONES*

On June 6, 2020, I was damn near skipping down Clifton Place in Bed-Stuy. The sun was shining, or maybe it wasn't, but everything about the moment felt perfect. I was smiling. I felt light. Euphoric.

My earbuds were pumping the heavy synths and minor chords of The Weeknd's "Blinding Lights" into my ears and spirit.

In that moment, the song belonged to me. It was my theme music as I bounced along the path I'd walked hundreds of times from Nostrand Avenue to Fort Greene, my wandering journey of choice. For those twenty minutes, I felt like a superhero. I felt like a non-failure. Not quite like a success, but also not like pure unreleased potential as I'd felt for most of my life to that point.

I was spinning in pure joy, and I won't pretend like I felt something else. There was a bit of fear mixed in, but that was the fear of being seen: the low hum of dread that comes from stepping out of obscurity. The fear I felt was separate from the unbridled terror and rage sweeping over most of our country at the time.

I was bubbling because a piece I'd written and submitted to the *New York Times* was published in print that morning, the day after it was published digitally, creating an online uproar. The piece had been headlined "I Don't Need 'Love' Texts from My White Friends" by the *Times*. (My original title was "Don't Send Love, Send Money.") It was my personal reaction—instructive, cheeky, and snarling—to white people texting me to offer their sympathies for the George Floyd tragedy, assuring me that they were "with me," whatever that meant. They wanted me to know they were on the side of the good guys. They wanted to check off the box for their good deed for the day. And I wanted nothing to do with their condolences. I wanted them to know that the best thing—the only thing—they could do to help as far as I could see was to sacrifice something for us that actually mattered to them. Their money.

When the piece was published, I felt what we've monikered "virality" for the first time. For twenty-four hours I felt like I was at the center of the internet; the center of the universe. I watched my Instagram follower count grow by thousands in mere hours. I watched friends, family members, strangers, and former colleagues joust in the comments under the piece when I posted it on my socials. I saw clips of Tucker Carlson on his Fox show calling me a Black Lives Matter radical and trying to trick his audience into thinking I was instructing white would-be allies to abandon their families for the sake of Black people. Spike Lee, a distant mentor, whom I hadn't heard from in months, called me to let me know that he had read the piece in print with his morning coffee. "You're the new Vanguard," he told me. "I'm proud of you."

The piece was a snowball growing in size and impact and re-posts every minute, and I bathed in it. I responded to many texts from Black friends and friends of color. I went into character, responding with the sort of understated humility that I thought was required of a writer in such a moment of national chaos. I performed gravity, maturity. But inside I felt like a little kid who was being told he was good enough for the first time. I felt validated as a writer. I had accessed the ever-elusive zeitgeist. I felt famous for those few days.

But the most compelling feeling, the one I cared about the most then and the one that still matters most to me in any creative victory was relief. I thought I was finally going to be rich.

George Floyd was dead, strangled to death by a policeman for being Black. Black people everywhere were protesting, putting their lives on the line because their frustration and sadness about police brutality and the unending anti-Blackness in our country had boiled over. We are so patient, but in this moment, Black folks had had enough. And, as if I need to remind you, we were all also living through the early, terrifying months of a pandemic. The Brooklyn streets I walked that day were emptier than I'd ever seen them in my ten years living in the city. All over our country, our world, people were panicking, fleeing, burning, fighting, dying, arguing. Overcrowded hospitals were turning dying people away in their last moments. Families were watching loved ones fade away on FaceTime because they couldn't expose themselves to the virus.

And I was skipping down the street.

Because I had been published in a prestigious journal and the world now knew I could write. And I had a book coming out just a few months later about lessons learned from surviving Blackness. I was watching the stars align around my subject matter in a way that was sure to make my book a hit when it came out in February, Black History Month. The tragedies of the moment offered a promising marketing and word-of-mouth advantage for my product. People were talking about Black stuff nonstop. Companies were seeking literature to buy to show their employees that they were "committed" to improving race relations within their companies. Media outlets were looking for voices, experts on Black life, to feed to their audiences and stir buzz and clicks and advertisement sales. A feeding frenzy for "Black content" that had begun years prior was now reaching a fever pitch.

None of that escaped me. I came from a corporate background, *the most* corporate background. Big tech. I came from an industry obsessed with capitalizing on people at their most vulnerable. An industry known to hire behavioral psychologists to help it seize on people's moments of fear, loneliness, and dread by offering products that give temporary hits of dopamine followed by *even lower* moments of fear, loneliness, and dread. I came from the industry that labels the people who engage with its products *users*, just as drug dealers do. I'm saying that I was keenly aware that this swell of national rage and fear around racial conflict in the middle of a pandemic created a unique opportunity for me as someone selling a product centered in Blackness. I had the product, and the world was bending to offer me users. And I was clocking it as it played out because that's what I'd learned to do from my days working in Silicon Valley. When people are hurting the most, that's when you arrive with your magical product that promises to cure the hurt. That's what I learned from the white boys in hoodies.

Chaos is a ladder.

A storm was brewing to feed my selfish ambitions to make money. I reveled in it as The Weeknd sang in my ears. I was giddy. As a Brooklyn-dwelling creative in my early thirties, I had seen countless trending activists and artists get STUPID rich by selling Instagram posts and books and TV series and clothes and magazines and trinkets and speaking engagements and anything and everything they could put their face on as demand for race-tragedy Band-Aids swelled. I began to know merchants of social agenda merchandise. I'll name them again: *trending activists.* Looters in the riot. I ran into them at parties and Soho House, at Netflix's corporate office in LA and Greenlight Bookstore in Fort Greene.

I judged them for their duplicity. They were media entrepreneurs branding themselves as agents of social change. After all, I was more righteous, I thought, more honest—a creative selling media. My name tag matched my intentions and my actions. I was writing books and TV pilots and movies, doing my best to sell them, and making my living doing so. I made a healthy living, enough to rent comfortably in New York City, but not much more.

The *trending activists* were the ones getting rich. I wore the same clothes everywhere, all the time: a wide-neck, long-torsoed black T-shirt from Urban Outfitters, black Nike joggers, and sneakers or black boots. But these people wore designer clothes, expensive jewelry, and makeup. I lived in a one-bedroom apartment in Bed-Stuy. These kids lived everywhere. Many had an apartment in Los Angeles, another in New York, another in their hometown, be it Houston or Baltimore or Chicago.

I had accrued a small audience on Instagram and Twitter for my work, a few thousand followers all told. As much as I wish it weren't so, those numbers matter in my business, and I keep constant observation over them (as we all do). "What's your social following?" I got accustomed to this constant refrain from executives and producers when I was a newcomer off the street hoping to sell a TV pilot or book proposal. It feels demeaning. It makes me feel like a widget for sale. Today, thankfully, they don't ask in the meeting anymore. But I know they check beforehand to see if I have a blue check. Barf. Sorry.

Back then I didn't have that kind of *verification*, so I always needed someone else with a larger platform to vouch for me. Those trending activists needed no such thing. Many carried the weight of hundreds of thousands—or even millions—of internet followers who they could sell as audience when peddling their faces and docu-series and other media products to studios and other such overlords. I saw many of them make millions of dollars doing so. I saw contracts. I saw numbers. And I saw them become rich, urban bourgeoisie who looked down on people who weren't in their club. I had one foot in their club because I was an actual creative, someone valuable to them because they could capitalize on me. They could use me to help them tell their stories of activism in a way that painted them as heroes. That gave me just enough of a window into their rich, fancy private lives to see that they were, indeed, raking in money in media sales, sponsorships, speaking fees, and merchandise.

I became jealous.

I used to run into one of the more famous trending activists at the Netflix office on Sunset Boulevard in Los Angeles. I was there often, trying, mostly unsuccessfully, to sell TV series and movies. The trending activist was there for the same reason—to do business. But his activism had bought him late-night talk show appearances and a following of millions on social media. That made him an attractive business partner for Netflix, who wanted the people tracking his activist journey to pay for subscriptions. The last time I saw him there, I noticed that he was on a first-name basis with Netflix co-CEO Ted Sarandos, as well as with a few of the celebrities who passed through the lobby. He always looked so comfortable there. Like he belonged. Legs crossed, pleasant, patient. He was always friendly to me, but I was still seeking the financial stability that he, presumably, had already achieved.

I remember thinking I must've looked how I felt: in a rush to sell my next project so I could pay my rent for a few more months.

"Are you doing okay?" he'd ask me as we dapped in the lobby with a giant digital display advertising Aziz Ansari's upcoming season of *Master of None* behind my head. The TA's words weren't just a pleasantry. I think he saw strain on my face. Maybe he could see I was hustling, spending dozens of hours writing new pilot ideas, spending the little money I had to fly back and forth from New York to LA to pitch them to execs who always said thanks but no thanks. I don't think he meant any harm in asking how I was doing, but I sensed a little condescension. He was telling me with his voice that we both knew I'd chosen the wrong profession. Writing was a long, grueling, lonely, competitive, and unlikely road to money and access. But the TA, well, the difference between our lifestyles was as clear as the contrast between his tailored Gucci pants and my thirty-dollar jeans.

Me and the TA ran into each other again at a housewarming in Brooklyn after he'd landed a first look deal at a major studio. How did he do that, I wondered. Could he write a screenplay? Had he ever produced a movie? Did he know how to direct? No, he said. But he had an audience. He had *followers*.

"But I'm not building a media company," he assured me.

It was then I realized what he and most of the trending activists were up to. Despite what they said, they *were* building media companies. Instagram and TikTok and Twitter were their direct-to-audience content platforms. Their lives, their voices and opinions and seething, accusatory meanness in public forums aimed sometimes at people on *their side of the issues*, was their product. They had made their lives into TV shows streaming on their social media channels, and their advertisers were all the litany of sponsors paying them to wear their clothes and donating money to their various nonprofit organizations and consulting firms. And they were raking in cash. They vacationed and partied and brunched with studio heads and corporate CEOs.

And I was jealous of them. Because more than I wanted their reach, their smugness, the deference they received from the people around them, their calm in places like the Netflix lobby and the Soho House, places where I feel so uncomfortable and unnerved and surrounded by sociopaths that I want to give myself a lobotomy . . . more than I wanted any of that, I wanted the money they had.

And I'd never felt closer to that type of money and success than I did when I wrote that piece about the absolute pain and dread of George Floyd's murder and sold it to the *New York Times*. I rejected then, and continue to reject now, the label of activist. I don't want that responsibility. I don't want that pigeonhole. I am not an activist; I *am* selling media.

But I was very happy to be trending. I had seen what trending had done for the rich, young *voices of change* around me. I could smell the money as the country was burning down. I had taken the pill this capitalist country offered me every moment my entire life: I let myself believe money could protect me from *being* George Floyd. The allure of money became for me a purpose that superseded all other reasons for being.

And now the pot of gold felt near. I could almost touch it. It glowed. It was blinding.

8

"Welcome to the Neighborhood."

As I make more money, I want to live close enough to white people to feel safe, and far enough from white people to feel safe. What I'm really saying is that I want to live in areas that aren't neglected by the state—under-resourced and abandoned, the way many Black neighborhoods are. But living in whiter areas and spending my time in whiter gyms, grocery stores, and restaurants shortens my breath. I become self-conscious about how much space I'm taking up, or not taking up. I become paranoid—is someone disrespecting me? Is the server at the restaurant taking longer to wait my table than the others surrounding it? I wonder if I'm being too direct with my trainer in the gym. Will I hurt his feelings? Will he tell the other trainers I'm a difficult client, that I'm aggressive? I wonder if he's using slang with me because I'm Black or if that's just how he talks. These are thoughts that pull me away from being present, from the natural, grounded flow of life. Living in those thoughts feels like living in a cloud; it makes it hard to see what's actually happening around me. It makes life opaque, and I can't afford that. I need to see clearly to write. I need to see clearly to earn my livelihood.

But I've let myself believe that living closer to whiteness offers me access to the state protection and amenities available to my white neighbors and counterparts. Every time a Black person is killed in a Black place, the idea that whiteness equals safety is reinforced in my head. Never mind the day-to-day suffocation of being the lone Black person in a white place. Staying alive takes precedence, and I've suffered losses that reinforce the idea that I might just have to suck it up and live in a white place to avoid what happens in *Black* places. To be clear, I think this is a miscalculation on my part. It's dangerous to be Black most places on earth. But you might see how I could land on the idea of living near whiteness as a preventative measure against dying for being Black.

In 2017, my friend Carrington Carter was shot and killed at the age of twenty-seven in Fort Washington, Maryland. I went to college with Carrington. Less than three years later, my friend Adam "Junior" Fongyen was shot and killed nine miles north in Northwest Washington, DC. Junior and I were high school basketball teammates. Fort Washington and Northwest Washington are known as *upwardly mobile* Black communities. I always think of the term *upwardly mobile* as a backhanded compliment levied on Black people with LinkedIn pages, one that disregards the rest of us as what? Downwardly mobile? Immobile?

When I lose friends to violence in Black areas—even, or maybe especially, "upwardly mobile" ones—I tell myself another convenient story. I tell myself that if these guys had moved into whiter neighborhoods, they would have been safer. I tell myself that it's worth being condescended to by white neighbors, spoken over by white colleagues, and occasionally mistaken for the service staff by white people at my gym, if it means that I'll get to stay alive.

But I've seen enough friends test this theory to know otherwise. Just last year, four armed gunmen followed my friend to his house in the Sherman Oaks neighborhood of LA in the middle of the night. He was able to speed away from the attempted robbery, but shots were fired at his car. My friend is Black, but Sherman Oaks is a 74 percent white neighborhood. It's a place where rich white people live just outside of Los Angeles.

The median price of a house in Sherman Oaks was $1.6M in 2023. It's a place where a Black person might buy a very expensive house and security system so she can feel safe from armed robbery and firearms. If we aren't safe there, and we aren't safe in Fort Washington, where are we safe?

The answer I give myself to calm my nerves is to earn more money, to move into an even safer neighborhood, with more security appliances.

But I know better. Money can't buy me safety. I know because I tried to buy it.

My then fiancée and I fled to my grandmother's retirement community in rural Maryland when Covid crushed New York City. That was our respite from Brooklyn, which was dense and dying. We were lucky to have anywhere at all to run off to in such an urgent and terrifying time.

When the virus loosened its grip on our city just slightly, we moved back to Bed-Stuy to see what life would become. We bought a German shepherd puppy to keep us company because she was adorable and we weren't sure if we'd ever again have a social life with humans.

The early months of the pandemic were emotionally difficult. But we felt fortunate because two scripted projects I'd been pitching in the months prior were picked up by studios and my partner kept her job at *Vice* while much of the company was laid off around her. The money afforded us the opportunity to move to a sparkling new building in Forest Hills, Queens.

The unit itself was spacious by New York apartment standards, and it had two balconies, one extending from the bedroom and the other from the living room. We had a dishwasher. For New Yorkers, this felt luxurious. Forest Park was just a three-minute walk from the building and offered a wooded oasis in the middle of noisy, dirty Queens. We were just ten minutes outside of Brooklyn, but I felt like we'd moved to another state.

There were reminders, of course, that we were still right there in New York City. For instance, one day we walked a few blocks down to pick up dinner from a Latin restaurant called Tu Casa where we saw a woman huddled in the corner of the restaurant smoking from a glass pipe. The restaurant staff and the patrons inside went about business as though nothing was happening at all. Thereafter, I referred to the restaurant as "Tu Crack Casa" every time we ordered their rice and beans and empanadas.

But for the most part, this neighborhood appeared pretty, charming, and safe. Besides the mix of modern and pre-war apartment buildings, there were single-family houses with giant yards and fancy-looking gates that reminded me of the rich suburban neighborhoods in Bethesda and Potomac, Maryland, where I'd valeted as a teenager. But these houses—sitting on half an acre in the middle of New York City—were an enormous flex. There was a welcoming, authentic Italian restaurant on our block, and we could walk ten minutes to a well-kept dog park and playground where kids played baseball and soccer. There were families here, and older people who hadn't yet been pushed out by gentrification as they had been on Clifton Avenue, where I'd lived in Bed-Stuy before. But this was a whiter neighborhood, although still diverse compared to most areas in the United States.

At night the streets around our apartment were empty and silent. I had never heard crickets at night in ten years of living in Manhattan and Brooklyn.

This was a step "up" for us, albeit a modest one. We had become "upwardly mobile," I guess. We were moving into a nice neighborhood with a bit more space, nice parks, and less-crowded sidewalks where we could walk our puppy. This felt like a place we could decompress and wait out the pandemic and be comfortable and learn how to be a family. And we were paying for it, $2,750 per month and the cost of gas for our used two-seat Jeep Wrangler. We named her Rocky.

We were paying for a little freedom from stress. It was a heavy expenditure, and I don't regret that decision, even considering what would come next.

Forest Park itself is over five hundred acres of grass, trees, and woods, with a floating breeze that ruffles the leaves almost enough to drown out the sound of cars rushing down the Jackie Robinson Parkway.

It's the kind of park that can take you away from New York City for an hour. I have a New Yorker friend who calls me "nature boy" because I grew up in Cub Scouts and I love being outside with the trees and the animals. I'm the designated fire builder on trips to Woodstock and bachelor parties in the Poconos. I'm the one who will pick up a small animal or insect, identify it to the group, and place it in a safer area while my friends make gagging faces.

So it was a source of peace for me, in this scary, chaotic moment, to live across the street from a vast, lush expanse where I could take our little shepherd puppy on long walks and pretend that I was back in the woods in Maryland or somewhere else where you can hear crickets and see stars at night.

One of the major differences between those places and this park, however, is that there is usually a stream of dog-walkers, hikers, and joggers making their way along the main path in Forest Park during the day. They were, for the most part, welcome company. But this was still New York City, after all, and our new neighbors had warned me that the park could be dangerous—particularly at night. So one day, at 10:30 in the morning, a few months after we'd moved, I took Penny Rihanna—six months old at the time—out for a walk. There were dozens of strollers rolling by. I felt safe.

I'd noticed a new phenomenon in my life when I took walks with our puppy: When I was with Penny, white people spoke to me. All the time. They'd smile and ask how old she was, ask if they could pet her—or just help themselves to a rub without asking. Some would kneel down beside her, rub her little face, and bask while she licked their mouths. I don't do that, but I guess if that's someone's thing, why not let them?

So on this walk, when a fiftyish white man, about 5'9" with a graying beard, got off his bicycle and stopped me to chat about Penny, I wasn't surprised. Penny was about forty-five pounds at this point, and only one of her shepherd ears had grown to point upward; the other still flopped to the side. It would be another month or so before she grew to a size where people saw her as a *dog*, one that could bite them.

This middle-aged guy, let's call him Gary, was wearing a college sweatshirt—I wish I could remember which—and had the affect of a Cornell professor. He was pleasant, with safe, kind eyes. He introduced himself by complimenting my adorable animal and welcoming us to the neighborhood. I mirrored him. I smiled. I was friendly. We'd only moved ten minutes outside of Brooklyn, but I felt like we were in a pseudo-suburb. I'm from the suburbs of Maryland, so I reached back into that side of me and made small talk with the guy, changing my tone of voice to appear unthreatening and assuring him—though he hadn't asked—that Penny did not bite. The truth is, at that point as a teething puppy, she very much did bite, but the damage was always negligible.

Gary gushed about the park's amazing, winding maze of wooded paths off the main drag. He said that if I hiked deep enough, I would find myself in a wonderland of trees, rare birds, horse trails, and unblemished nature. That sounded like exactly what I needed. *Nature boy.* And as I got to know that park over the following year, it turned out his description was mostly true.

Gary offered to be our tour guide, to walk us through the wooded labyrinth deep into the park, off the main trail. I took him up on the offer, enthusiastically, even. I trusted him. A stranger. I'm surprised I made that choice considering how coiled and cynical I can be when white people offer kindness. I'm usually searching for the hidden ulterior motive behind their niceness. But coiling that way all the time makes me rigid and sore. It's isolating to watch white people so closely, all the time, with such intensity and skepticism. It's exhausting to think so hard all the time about how they might betray me or humiliate me or hurt me.

I recently went alone to a Gary Clark Jr. show at Red Rocks Amphitheatre in Denver, Colorado. I waited in line in the pouring rain beside a small, delightful group of white fans who had driven eight hours from rural Iowa to watch their favorite artist. Together, we hid under a boulder from the storm and talked about how much rain we were willing to endure to see the artist. I'm not a huge fan, but I was there for the experience. They were so sweet—two guys and a lady—and earnest. They offered me water and cigarettes and an opportunity to join their group for the duration of the show. They told me about Iowa and how there wasn't much going on in their town besides garage bands and drinking out in the cornfields. They were wearing camo and trucker hats. The guys were stout with long bushy beards. As we spoke, my subconscious whispered to me about what their politics might be and what they might think of me, this Black guy with long locks alone in the Denver mountains.

But I ignored the voice and focused on connecting with these people and mirroring their kindness. As we moved to our seats, we lost each other. I ended up watching the show beside a couple in their early twenties—an Asian man and a white woman—who couldn't have been sweeter. I enjoyed the performance, and the venue itself is the best I've ever experienced. But I couldn't help notice the almost entirely white audience getting drunker and clumsier in their movements as the show went on. I eyed the exits. When the set seemed near the three-quarter mark, I began the long walk toward the rideshare lot to avoid ending up alone in the drunken rush of white fans making their way out of the amphitheater.

When I made it to the parking lot, a white guy in his early thirties struck up a conversation with me. He spoke like a college-educated urbanite. He had piercings in his face. He was slim, wearing a black vest adorned with pins. He told me he had moved to Denver from Austin, and that most people our age in Denver were transplants. He mentioned that he'd always wanted to go to New York, but he'd never been. And he offered me a ride back downtown. Hesitantly, I accepted his offer because I didn't want to dismiss his generosity and because an Uber would've cost about a hundred dollars. We walked and chatted, and I asked him to point out his car. He showed me a large, black pickup truck thirty feet away from us. Something about the vehicle scared me. My cynicism kicked in. I imagined myself tied up somewhere two hours outside of Denver in a basement where this guy and his friends did their Saturday-night thing to me. Whatever that may be.

My friend Isaac, who I was staying with, worked as a security guard at a nightclub until three a.m. I wouldn't be able to reach him if I needed help. I stopped walking toward the car. The guy looked back at me.

"I'm sorry, man. I'm just gonna take an Uber," I said.

"You sure?" he asked.

"Yeah," I responded. "I think I gotta do that."

He didn't push it. His eyes showed disappointment, but he nodded and walked away. He understood that I was being cautious, and I think he understood that I should be. Maybe that moment cost me a friendship, or a nice conversation, or another reason to love Denver. But that's what those voices that tell me to distrust white people and their acts of apparent kindness do. I don't fault myself for having those voices. They were forged by experience and history.

But it's a big burden to always be on defense. It blocks connection, which is vital to me. So sometimes I give myself a break and let myself trust white people. I let myself trust Gary.

Gary, on his bike, turned into the woods down a narrow path between bushes while Penny and I trailed him on foot, always about ten feet behind. As we made it about fifty yards into the woods, I could no longer see the stream of joggers on the main path. The thick brush beside us and the towering trees above us created a shade that started to make me feel lost. The early seeds of panic began to take root. I dismissed them. I just can't live so paranoid all the time.

I considered "accidentally losing" my tour guide. I slowed my pace but worried I might not be able to find our way out of the park. And Gary was keeping an eye on me and Penny. Whenever we lagged by more than twenty feet, Gary would stop on his bike, look back, and wait for us. I wanted to believe he was just being a thoughtful guide, trying not to let us get lost in this complex web of trees and trails and bushes. But something in my gut didn't feel right. He seemed just a bit *too* concerned with our whereabouts. I felt trapped in the woods and trapped in my head negotiating with my paranoia.

One hundred yards into the maze, I started noticing used condoms and empty beer cans scattered in the dirt. Now I was on high alert.

Gary noticed me noticing the condoms. "Teenagers," he said with a smile and a shrug. I smiled back at him, and he continued to lead us into the woods.

I was creeped out.

But I was a grown man with a dog in the woods just a few blocks from my home in the middle of the day. Why should I be afraid?

After a dozen more yards, Penny planted her front paws into the ground, barked, and pulled at her leash. I swiveled my head around to see what was wrong. I saw nothing but trees and bushes. I heard nothing but rustling leaves and the crunch of Gary's bike up ahead, but I couldn't see him anymore. I turned a corner following the sound of Gary's bike, all but dragging Penny along at this point.

Then I saw something really scary. I saw what Penny must have known was there when she started pulling in the opposite direction. It was a man standing about 6'4", who had to weigh three hundred pounds, in a black tank top and his underwear. He had olive skin and two long gray braids that stretched halfway down his back. He was frozen, staring, towering, a dozen feet away. He had spotted me first. He didn't budge and neither did I. Penny barked frantically. The man just stared. He had cold, hollow, deep-set eyes that warned me to get away.

I didn't know how to do that. If I turned my back, he might take me down. If I walked backward, I might stumble and fall. I thought about releasing Penny's leash so she could run and do who knows what. Find help? Attack the man?

Gary emerged between us and the man. He looked unconcerned, still as pleasant as ever. He beckoned with his head for Penny and me to follow him down the trail away from the man, and we did, this time staying right by his side. I was relieved. I felt safer than I did moments ago, but I was still confused. Gary seemed completely unfazed.

"What was that?" I asked.

"Oh, you know, people come into the park for privacy," Gary said. "He wasn't gonna bother us."

Now I knew I needed to get out of the woods. Gary's vibe was much too casual. How could Gary not be spooked by that giant guy doing who-knows-what in the middle of these woods? My tone became serious and insistent. I was panicking.

"I think we should head back," I said. "I have work to do."

"Oh, but we're just about to see the best part," Gary protested.

"Yeah, but it's time. Thanks for showing us around," I said.

"We're almost there."

He was telling me: "No. We are not leaving yet." I understood what Gary had known all along: There was no way I could find my way back from here.

Gary stopped us near the top of a hill in a clear spot beneath the canopy where we could see far out across the woods. If anyone approached, we'd see them before they saw us.

I stood, gripping Penny's leash firmly as Gary parked his bike. He took his time with each motion. This seemed routine for him. In my head I ran back over my decision to follow this man this deeply into this park without knowing how to get out. We were his prisoners. That much was clear.

He smiled at me and said some trifling things about the beauty of the park. We stood feet apart. Now he looked like he was holding in excitement. His hands were unsteady.

And then.

"You know, you're a really attractive man," Gary said.

Fuck. I was paralyzed. I thought to myself, if only Penny were bigger and could understand what was happening. But then again, I wasn't yet sure what was happening. She was panting, looking off into the woods.

I made myself small. I wondered if he had a weapon. His forehead was sweaty. He was wobbly on his feet like he couldn't control himself. But he didn't touch me.

"You're the kind of guy a guy like me could just . . . ," he said. Then he paused and sort of made this shuddering, drooling noise. It was gross.

He asked me to have sex with him. I told him I didn't want to. I added that I was engaged to a woman. I'm still not sure why I added that detail. I thought maybe it would back him off.

"That's a shame," he responded.

His tone was commanding and threatening. And disgusting. And self-satisfied.

I continued to decline his advances in a passive, almost charming way. I seriously thought he might try to hurt me or kill me. He asked me one more time if I was sure that I didn't want sex. I was definitive in my response, but still gentle. I was still trying not to scare him.

I was stronger and in much better shape than he was. I could have beat his ass. Or worse. Both me and Penny could have easily outrun him, but maybe he had a gun. I made sure to make sure he knew that I knew he was the boss. He was in power.

My decision was calculated. I was choosing life over dignity.

This was the fall of 2020.

Just a few short months after George Floyd was murdered by

police officer Derek Chauvin. That was the same day Amy Cooper, a white woman, lied to the police about the actions of Christian Cooper (a Black man, no relation) in an effort to sic them on him. In my view, and the views of many others, that was a repulsive attempt on Christian's life and it played out in Central Park just ten miles away from where I was trapped with Gary.

I would have to write another entire book—probably several volumes—to recount all the millions of the other data points that would lead me, a Black person in the woods, to know that fighting or calling the police on Gary was no option. If authorities showed up to find that something violent happened between us, I'd face consequences. Gary, a middle-aged white guy, would be defended, and absolved.

What I'm saying is that I was out of options. I'm trying to get out in front of this. I'm defending myself, because people will judge me for my choices in the moment—to avoid conflict as best I could. But what else could I do? Gary wanted sex from me. I was unwilling. I couldn't run because he wouldn't let me go. I had seen his face so clearly. I knew his voice. I knew he frequented this park. For all I knew, he had a weapon, and if I ran, he might use it on me. Then he'd tell the "authorities" I provoked him. I couldn't call the police because inviting them would only put me in more danger. And I couldn't fight because the story would be "Black man, early thirties, with German shepherd beats up an old, rich, white guy in the woods." And there would be my photo: Black skin, dreadlocks, looking hardly older than my mid-twenties.

I had been tricked into following this man deep into the woods by his false kindness. I still question how I could have been so naïve.

Now I just wanted to get out alive. I told him as much.

"I really want to go," I said. "Can you just tell us how to get out of here?"

"Okay, I will. I just have to pee. Will you keep a lookout?" Gary asked.

I said that I would and started to think that maybe I had gotten off easy. I was still on edge, of course, but it seemed like he'd finally accepted that I didn't want anything to do with him. He stepped behind a tree about eight feet away. I waited for a minute or so and didn't hear any urine stream. Then he started talking to me.

"You really are a very good-looking man," he said. I peeked over and realized he was looking at me. I looked away fast.

"I'm almost done, sorry, I had a lot of water," he lied.

Another thirty seconds passed. I've tried since that day to find a way around the truth. But here it is: Gary was standing there by the tree looking right at me and masturbating. He let out these tired, repulsive moans while he did it.

Then he zipped up his pants and hopped back on his bike.

Now what, I wondered.

Then, I heard a beautiful sound. It was the sound of children laughing and chattering. Two preschool teachers were leading a group of children through the woods. The babies were tied together adorably by little ropes as they often are on these sorts of walks in New York City. They were too far away to see us, but I was overcome with relief to know that someone, anyone, was within earshot.

But I was still scared and in shock, too nervous to yell out to the teachers. Gary still seemed calm. He said he would lead us back to the main path so that me and Penny could go home. We followed him. As soon as he reached a point in the woods where we could see the path, I thanked him for showing us the way back. I did so pleasantly. I fucking thanked him.

I wanted to make sure he wasn't worried that I was going to try to report him to the police or whatever. He smiled.

"Welcome to the neighborhood," he said. He said it like he had just brought a pan full of brownies to our front door. He followed up by saying he'd see me around the park. I wasn't sure if it was a throw-away statement or a threat to keep my mouth shut. I took it as something in between.

He rode away on his bike. I watched him go, making sure he didn't see which way I went to head home. As people and dogs passed us on both sides, I just stared after Gary.

I took a long winding route back to our apartment with Penny, just in case he tried to follow. His leering and threatening and propositioning was in my head now. It was in my imagination too.

For months thereafter, I avoided that big, beautiful park on my walks with Penny. He had clouded my oasis. I was afraid every time my then fiancée went to the same park for her own walks. I told her what happened to me there, and she was empathetic and comforting. But she's tough, and she wasn't about to give up the park to Gary.

Forest Park was the main attraction for our new family to move into that neighborhood. We had paid for it. It was expensive. And in forty-five minutes, Gary made me afraid of that place. He lured me with fake kindness. And in the moment of truth, he was protected by whiteness. I couldn't defend myself by pitting my word against his. I couldn't call for defense from the police. He had control because he was white and I am Black. I wasn't so afraid of what he might do to me, but what I might do to him to defend myself, and what that might cost me.

I shared this story with my then fiancée and one other woman I trusted. They assured me that what happened was sexual assault. They also made sure to remind me that these are the sorts of interactions women deal with constantly.

When I tell others or myself this story, I always get shy about using that language. The word *assault* makes me feel like a victim. It makes me feel helpless, like he was a wolf and I was a sheep. It makes me feel like I didn't have choices.

Among other reasons, I wanted to move out of Brooklyn to this neighborhood to feel a little bit safer. To be outside the fray. And within months, I was assaulted. Something that *never* happened to me when I lived in Brooklyn, in Harlem, in Oakland, or in West Atlanta.

Months went by. On my walks around the neighborhood with Penny, I always looked over my shoulder to see if Gary was watching. After five months or so, the anxiety faded, and I returned to the park. I still avoided the side trails. I walked alone down the main pathway among the dozens of joggers and strollers. I looked up at the trees and felt the sunlight on my face and let myself wander through nature. That's probably my favorite thing to do.

On one such day, while the sun warmed my cheeks, I felt eyes on me. I looked down the path and noticed Gary standing on the side with his bike. I kept my pace toward him, pretending I didn't see him, but he knew. He waited, and as I got within earshot, he smiled his self-satisfied smile and waved for my attention. "Hey, Chad," he said. I forced a smile back so I didn't raise any alarms. I wanted so badly to never see him again. I didn't speak, but I gave him just enough recognition to make sure he knew we didn't have a problem. I kept walking, right past him.

I took thirty more paces before looking back to see if he was watching me. He was gone.

Gary was able to get away with what he did because there was a power imbalance between us. Only he can know how consciously he wielded that power, but I never stopped thinking about it throughout our entire interaction. That's the enormous power of white supremacy: It took over my thoughts entirely, while Gary likely ignored it altogether throughout our interaction. He was focused on preying, and he could lean on his whiteness to do so without even realizing that was what he was doing. Meanwhile, I was focused on escaping without threatening him. And even still, I could never prove that Gary's race gave him leverage in the woods to anyone who refused to believe it.

So Gary rides away on his bike to wait in the bushes for the next person like me to amble across his path. For him to get what he wants, he'll have to find them in a moment when they're willing to suspend their cynicism for some reason. The reason for me was that I had made some money and spent some money to live in a place that I wanted to believe was safe. I wanted to believe it was a place where even the white people would treat me with respect, a place where I could trust them—as neighbors, as friends, even. Gary did well to dampen whatever hope I had left for that sort of interaction . . . And yet, I still hope that somewhere, in some neighborhood, those conditions can exist.

But Gary is gone. My life moved on and I barely think about that day. If I am angry and sad about what happened there, I've buried those feelings deeply enough that I can no longer feel them. As I recount the story now, I feel detached and curious and a little introspective. I wonder why I let that happen. It seems so often the case that when white people injure me emotionally, I have no means for retribution besides this. Besides writing about it so that people like me know to beware of people like Gary, and so that people like Gary know the damage they cause to people like me.

9

Lost in Space

There are times when I think I write so sharply about race so that white people will see me coming. My thought is that if they know from my writing that I see them clearly, or even just that I am seeing them with an intent to chronicle their behaviors toward me, that they will offer their best behavior or their deference. I've seen this play out. Not long after I published my first book, *Black Magic*, Julie Bowen of *Modern Family* fame reached out to me. Julie had also read my post–George Floyd op-ed in the *New York Times*. Both the book and the op-ed spoke bluntly about the racism I've encountered around white friends, coworkers, and associates.

Julie complimented my writing and thought there might be a way we could work together. We struck up a chemistry over several long conversations, and I pitched her on a podcast concept I had been developing—*Quitters*—centered on conversations with people about what they'd left behind to start their *real* lives. The concept resonated with Julie, as she had experience quitting an eating disorder early in life and a marriage just a few years before we met. She was in.

I flew out to Hollywood to spend a week with Julie and our producer Rachael sorting out the flow of each episode and recording a few trial interviews. Julie offered to host me as a guest in her new house. Saving money by bunking in one of its many rooms was appealing. And I was excited to check out the cutting-edge recording studio in the guesthouse behind the pool. Julie's offer was generous, and now that I know her well, I know the offer was genuine. At the time, though, I was afraid to sleep in a white woman's house. This was, after all, just months after my run-in with Gary. I booked a room at the Universal City Hilton.

Julie was a consummate host who offered big energy and love from the moment I stepped inside until I left on our last day of recording. She gave me space, and advice when I wanted it, and a seemingly unlimited supply of Zevia canned drinks. I complimented her house and pretended not to marvel at its high ceilings, courtyard, swimming pool, and its tasteful rustic decor.

Each day we recorded an episode of our podcast with a guest from Julie's Rolodex. Jesse Tyler Ferguson. Ty Burrell. Carly Chaikin. Jimmy Kimmel. I felt a rush in these first interviews, figuring out how to format the show with Julie while learning our chemistry on the fly, all while trying to keep the guests engaged. I was always aware of the wide gulf between Julie's notoriety and mine. She managed the imbalance by gushing over my writing and highlighting to the guests that I was the "academic" in our partnership in addition to being the creator of the show. I didn't and don't think of myself as an academic, but I appreciated what Julie was doing, trying to create an eye-level experience between me and Julie and our famous guests.

As we opened each interview, Julie introduced me to the guests by mentioning my book and my *New York Times* op-ed, and a few of the guests were familiar with the op-ed. I saw a look of understanding wash over their faces. One, who I won't name, said she remembered reading my piece and feeling embarrassed by the fact that she'd done exactly what I railed against in the piece: In the wake of George Floyd, searching for something to do with her anxiety and shame, she texted her Black friends telling them she was sorry for their circumstance and assuring them they had no responsibility to respond to her. As I wrote in the piece, such gestures were exhausting and annoying to me. The people who sent those texts forced me into an impossible dual role, simultaneously casting me as a caretaker who could relieve their guilt *and* as a victim to be pitied. I included a specific text message I'd received from one friend that stood as an example of the type of outreach I didn't want. I quoted the text exactly but left out the friend's name. I was using the anecdote to make a point in my writing, but I was also sending a warning shot to create some space between me and other white friends who spoke to me in ways that made me feel uncomfortable. I was letting them know that violations might be captured and published. If you think that's unfair of me, well, I sometimes think so too. But other times I think my pen is my only defense against anti-Blackness, even in my friendships.

In the studio, I noticed our guest's face flush as she described her experience reading my piece. It had made her realize how insensitive and annoying she must have come across to her Black friends during that time. She was ashamed to have had such a blind spot. Recounting this, she looked embarrassed all over again. It had only been a year since the summer of 2020. The feelings were still fresh for all of us. We talked about my piece for a few minutes and then made a clumsy transition into our interview. Throughout it, I felt our guest retreat and defer to me not only in conversation, but also in body language and in tone. She seemed to be reeling from our conversation's starting place and from knowing that I was the sort of person who keeps a record of my experiences with people. It seemed she could tell that one day I'd be doing what I'm doing now: exploring our interaction publicly. She seemed like a nice and graceful person anyway, but I felt her giving me a profound amount of space as compared to Julie, with whom she shared a more even cadence.

At first, I liked all of that space. I liked feeling that my voice carried a weight. But midway into our hour-long conversation, I started to feel gluttonous. I love the sparks of friction in an honest, balanced conversation, and I found those sparks were missing because our guest was so cautiously staying out of my way. I started to feel like I was talking into the void. Our guest didn't want to say anything that might offend me, so she disappeared. My writing had scared her off and left me in space in this conversation. I thought such a power imbalance would feel like freedom, but instead I felt alone in an echo chamber.

After the interview we took photos together with the guest and she left. When Julie and I were alone, we postgamed the interview, and I mentioned to Julie that I felt the guest seemed reluctant to jump fully into conversation with me. Julie supposed that the guest may have been intimidated by me because of my bona fides as a writer. But I think there was more to it. I think she feared how I would write about our interaction later. That fear gave me space to express myself unfettered in our conversation. Some might call that space power. But I'm cautious.

On the one hand, I'm working furiously to grow my platform so that my writing reaches far and clears space for me around white people when I enter rooms like that studio. I need that space to push my point of view and create, and I also need it in order to make space for other people like me. I've felt that same sort of space in pitch meetings at studios with white executives, at meetings with agents and producers, with editors, with friends of friends at parties in Brooklyn.

When I finish speaking, I realize nobody has interrupted or pushed back with their own voice as goes the natural flow of conversation. I write intentionally so my point of view reaches others and precedes me with that space. But I don't know if that space is freedom or isolation. When I feel that twinge of gluttony I stop talking. I get quiet. I look at the people around me and await direction because I'm not used to being on that end of a power imbalance with white people. That makes me distrust the quiet, and then the space is filled with the sound of my own paranoia telling me to watch my step. And then the space is gone.

10

Profound Whiteness

When I enter a room full of white people, my breathing becomes restricted. I take smaller, tighter breaths that pull less oxygen into my body. That shallow chest-breathing—as opposed to diaphragmatic breathing—has a range of damaging short- and long-term effects on the body. But the immediate effect on me is that I become angry and sad. I recently visited a doctor to help me improve my sleep. After an hour or so in her chair having the inside of my throat photographed, I was told that the nasal passage to my throat is restricted because my tongue is too big for my mouth. So I wake up in the middle of the night after snoring loudly. Then I struggle to get back to sleep. My doctor said that's because my body thinks it's fighting for its life when oxygen is restricted, so it pumps in adrenaline to help with the fight. My heart rate goes up, my muscles tense.

My doctor is making me a special mouthpiece to help keep my

giant tongue out of my throat passage while I sleep. But what am I to do when my breathing is restricted because I feel crowded by whiteness?

I should be precise here. Not all rooms full of whiteness are alike. In the liberal-leaning spaces that I most frequently inhabit—the set of our *Quitters* podcast, Brooklyn, creative pockets of New York and Los Angeles—most of the white people I encounter try to make compensations for my lack of structural power by offering interpersonal power. Said more simply, these people try to avoid stepping on my voice, poking at me in anti-Black ways, and silencing me. I think their reasons for this sort of behavior vary; some are genuinely trying to be kind, and others are cynically trying to avoid being canceled or deemed bigoted. Regardless, I know that in those rooms I can lean into the extra space created by white people who want me to have that space. If that all sounds contrived and complicated, I promise that the rooms themselves feel even more tangled. But still, I sometimes appreciate the gesture to make me feel comfortable.

Of course, there are other white spaces where no such considerations are offered. There are places where white people want me to feel as small and restricted as possible. I suppose they don't even think there is any other way I *should* feel.

My partner and I traveled to South Florida in November 2022 to visit family for Thanksgiving. My assistant booked a room for us in the Grand Opus Resort in Delray, an hour's drive north from Miami. As we navigated our rental car through sparkling clean streets lined with palm trees and gaudy beach shops, I noticed that nearly everyone in this part of Delray was white, except for the Black and brown service workers emptying trash bags and carrying boxes into the back doors of the shops. They looked exhausted and beaten down.

The white vacationers looked happy. Stridently so. And they weren't just white—they were sort of profoundly white. Pastel polo shirts, khaki shorts, leather thong sandals, sun-strained skin that seemed to have spent plenty of time on fishing boats and golf courses. Straw hats. Sunburns.

I felt my breaths shorten and my chest tighten. I tried to continue talking with my then fiancée as though everything was okay, but I was drowning. I glanced at Google Maps, hoping we were farther away from the hotel than it showed. I wished we would turn onto some new street revealing a different environment, one equally close to the pristine beaches and sparkling, clear water of the Atlantic Ocean, but with Black and brown people enjoying this scenic backdrop as patrons, not laborers.

But I knew better. I stayed quiet and watched out the window as we passed dozens of small groups of gleeful, white faces.

I had made a terrible error by not double-checking the area around the resort to see if Black people were welcome there. As we pulled into the front of the resort, I mentioned that I'd prefer we not spend much time in the area around the hotel. My then fiancée agreed emphatically.

Once inside, the twentysomething white woman working at the front desk was chipper and friendly, extending herself to make us feel welcome and trying her best to hide her excitement at the novelty of us being there. As she checked us in, my head was on a swivel, taking in the lobby environment with its high ceilings, shimmering glass chandelier, and a mesmerizing fountain just inside the front door. I saw more white people wearing pastel polos and dresses; I saw no Black patrons.

I noticed two Black housekeepers sneak into a back closet behind the front desk. We made brief, deep eye contact. I was happy to see them. My breathing improved just a bit, but I was still bracing myself, so coiled, so tense. Throughout our stay, the service staffers who stopped by the room to offer housekeeping would linger in conversation with us, the only Black couple in the building as far as I saw. One told my then fiancée that she hated working in this hotel and wished she could spend Thanksgiving with her family instead of working. I thought of season 2 of HBO's *The White Lotus*, which is set on a resort in Italy and features a cast that includes no Black people: none as patrons in the resort, none as staff workers in the resort, none in the surrounding areas. Maybe they're all in the back, complaining about the pastel-wearing patrons. That would be a good show.

Anyway.

My then fiancée and I walked past the swimming pool on the way to the elevator. The pool had a stunning view of the beach just across the street. I love to swim. Every time we would walk past the pool on the way to and from the elevator, I'd look for just *one* Black face among the dozens of white patrons swimming, splashing, lounging, reading, enjoying the setting for which we'd all paid. I never saw one. I never saw *one* Black person in or around that pool. So I never went out there. Swimming is unpleasant when your breathing is restricted.

I forfeited whatever percentage of our booking fee went toward access to that pool because I knew it would suck to be out there, alone or with my partner, receiving judging and warning looks or overzealous, forced conversations.

After we'd spent a day in the Grand Opus, I decided that I didn't want to go into the café downstairs or the restaurant and bar. I felt watched and pushed. I noticed how bloated white men expanded their chests and shoulders as I entered the elevator or walked toward them and their families in the hallway. I'm Black, of medium build, with dreadlocks that hang past my shoulders. I wear a small gold chain. I have broad shoulders. I've developed a look, a stare, with a bit of a smirk behind it, that is meant to tell people in pastel shirts to keep our conversations brief.

On the second day of our trip, my partner and I stopped briefly in the lobby at the hotel shop so I could buy a pair of socks. The white woman at the register offered clipped conversation. She seemed unhappy, but not in a way that had anything to do with me. That was oxygen. She was the first white person I encountered in the hotel who didn't seem to care that I was there. Our interaction was meaningless to her, just a transaction. What a treat to get to spend my money on something I needed without paying a tax on it.

And then I felt him approach. A middle-aged white man in a pastel shirt and those khaki shorts—the uniform. He came from my right side, waddling a bit, taking up as much space as he pleased and letting us both know he was coming. He asked the cashier to fetch some item for him while she was still in the middle of our transaction. I didn't look at him. I held my face stiff and waited for him to get what he needed—at the expense of my time—and get the fuck on. But that wasn't enough for him.

The cashier found the item and handed it to the man.

"You're the best," he said.

"I know," she responded, deadpan.

It seemed they had met before. I continued to look straight ahead at the cashier, still not moving. The man leaned into my space.

"That's what he said," he quipped. I still don't even get the joke. If he wanted me to respond somehow, I refused. If he wanted to make me uncomfortable, he succeeded. On the outside, I was paralyzed. On the inside, I was enraged because now my time *and* my space were being seized. Without looking, I knew that a dozen other white people in pastels were within thirty feet of us.

If I turned and yelled at him to back the fuck up, would I make it out of Delray? Would I end up in jail? Would I end up in heaven?

But the idea of yelling at this man, or God forbid pushing him, is laughable because I've been so deeply programmed to accept this abuse from white people, white men especially. And no amount of money earned or spent on an expensive hotel room protects me from his bullshit.

So, I said nothing. And then . . .

"You know, I used to have hair just like his," he said. He was, of course, referring to my long dreadlocks, several of which are wrapped with light brown highlights.

He chuckled. Now, I wanted to commit a crime. But what I did was worse.

I snorted out a one-syllable, pseudo laugh. It came more from my nose than my mouth. I held eye contact with the cashier and still didn't look at him. But I gave him just enough of a reaction in that noise to give him a response, to make him feel let in, to acknowledge his position. I self-abandoned.

The cashier was aware of me. I can only imagine the number of times her dignity has been impinged on by a puffed-up little sun-drunk, middle-aged white guy at her register in that hotel. She gave the man the most understated smile. This tension she didn't ask for must have been a low point in her day. And I felt some responsibility for that.

The man kept going.

"Yeah, I used to have long, long hair! You wouldn't believe," he said. He didn't touch me, or my hair, but I thought he might. And I considered what I'd do. Again, the most unlikely reaction jumped to mind. I'd fling his hand away, push him onto the ground, and stand over him.

Yeah, right.

The cashier completed our transaction. I wished her a happy Thanksgiving.

I turned to the man finally. I made eye contact, and I said, "Happy

Thanksgiving." My shoulders and hips moved at stiff angles like a robot. I wanted to make sure I didn't do or say anything to reveal how I felt. I needed to escape this moment so my then fiancée and I could go downstairs to our rental car and make it to Thanksgiving dinner.

Back in the car that afternoon, my breathing returned to me. I could think. As my body came back to me, my first thought was to suggest that we move to a different hotel, one with Black patrons. My then fiancée understood where the feeling was coming from, but a hotel move would cost more money, time, and energy.

So we stayed in the Grand Opus. Each time we left family gatherings in other areas, we'd drive back to the parking lot under the hotel and make our way directly from the front door, past the swimming pool full of white bodies and faces, up to our room where we could breathe.

We never even went to the beach. And I'm a Pisces. I love the beach.

11

Jay-Z and the Owners

I need to be able to breathe *everywhere* I go. That's a basic need. But as previously discussed, there are places where I can't breathe easily, and that triggers fight-or-flight instincts that can ruin a moment, a day, a life. As a solution to that pesky problem of needing to breathe no matter where I am, I reach for *the money lie*. The Money Lie is that wicked product of capitalist and white supremacist propaganda that tells us money is the great equalizer. It tells us that money makes a Black person whiter, and thus, more adequate to receive the innate benefits of whiteness, e.g., oxygen, protection from harm, access to more money, and otherwise.

The Money Lie is especially wicked because it compounds on itself. It's well documented that when people get rich, they don't get happier or more fulfilled or truly confident. But even still, so many double down on money as the solution to all of life's problems. As a well-known producer once warned me in his G-Wagon driving through the Hollywood Hills, "We're all just a bunch of miserable rich guys trying to get richer but just getting more miserable."

By "we," he was referencing his cohort of mega-rich, Black producers whose lives were all consumed by getting richer. He was warning me that while the endless pursuit of money *might* make me rich, it would definitely make me unhappy. But at the time, The Money Lie was so deeply rooted in me that all I cared about was the exciting truth that I was now rubbing elbows with Hollywood rich folk. The Money Lie is so powerful that it blocked out my ability to take in this friend's warning. All I took away from that conversation, at the time and for years afterward, was confirmation that I was in the right rooms and should keep going back into those rooms until I was rich. Never mind the miserable part. The money could solve that, of course. That's what The Money Lie says. Money can solve everything.

And that brings me back to my space and breathing problem. The Money Lie promises that *if I just had more money, I'd be able to buy the space and the air I need no matter the environment.*

The Money Lie almost has me completely in its grip.

But then I think about Jay-Z.

Somewhere near the top of every NBA arena and NFL stadium there's something called an owner's box, a plush, well-appointed mega-suite complete with full bar, gourmet cooking services, and waitstaff. The owner's box looks out over the customers in the stands onto the court or field. This is where the almost entirely white, male, billionaire franchise owners sit with their mostly white, male guests to watch the mostly Black players who work for them compete and perform. Infrequently, the television broadcast will pan to the owner's box during a stoppage in play to offer viewers a shot of these men and their guests, usually all looking grumpy or shouting over the crowd into one another's ears. I've never sat in one of these boxes, but I imagine that they are telling some faux self-deprecating joke for the ninetieth time and that their guests feel obligated to laugh because, after all, the owner has given them the opportunity on this day to sit among the elite in wealth to watch the elite in talent put on a show.

I guess the TV broadcasts show the owner's boxes so infrequently because the men who inhabit them prefer to capitalize in quiet and because, generally speaking, I don't think most people want to watch a bunch of old, frumpy white guys do business. (Although, I suppose, *Succession* and its rack of Emmys prove otherwise.)

Every now and then, when the cameras pan up to the owner's box, I'll see a Black person in there sitting uncomfortably hunched beside one of the owners.

Sometimes the Black person sitting with the owners is Jay-Z, aka Shawn Carter. Jay-Z is so overassociated with the term *Black billionaire* that it's barely worth mentioning his fortune at all. But it's important for me to remember that he shares billionaire status with the owners when I see him up there in their boxes. And there's no doubt that his net worth is what gets him an invite from the owners despite his Black skin. And it doesn't hurt that his entertainment company, Roc Nation, has a multiyear deal with the NFL "to enhance the NFL's live game experience and to amplify the league's social justice efforts," according to a 2019 NFL press release. This is like the scaled-up, billionaire version of someone paying me a few thousand dollars to give a one-hour DEI talk at their corporation.

There are many reasons to criticize Jay-Z (not to mention the NFL), but we can all agree Jay-Z is a formidable musician, writer, and businessman, to say the least. He has a unique confidence that forces others to consider why *they* aren't just as confident. He never yells in interviews to get a point across. In fact, he sometimes speaks so softly that I have to turn up the volume on my phone to hear what he's saying. He can speak that quietly because he knows I *will* turn the volume up to hear what he's saying. He knows we all will. He's the person who conquered hip-hop as it rose to international prominence, as it became the most culturally influential music in the world. He and a small handful of others pioneered that *takeover*.

I was introduced to Jay-Z a few years ago in Dumbo, Brooklyn, at an after-party for his and Beyoncé's On The Run II Tour. He stands up tall in his 6'2" frame, with willowy arms at his sides. His gaze pierced me. He looked right down into me. I am not someone who likes to be made to feel small, but he did so without trying, I'm sure.

We exchanged only a few sentences. I told him I'm a fan, something I can't remember saying to anyone before or since. I didn't know what else to say.

I've of course met taller and heavier people, but I've never been around someone who felt bigger in presence. Some of that feeling is projection. I was thirteen years old when *The Blueprint* album dropped. "Heart of The City (Ain't No Love)" and "Renegade" were the first two rap songs I could recite word for word. I used to write the lyrics down on wide-ruled, loose-leaf pages in my Trapper Keeper binder during seventh-grade social studies classes. Then I'd stare at the words and behold how they all fit together so perfectly.

This is all to say that Jay-Z is gigantic in presence, physicality, and wealth.

But when the cameras pan to show Jay-Z sitting with the owners, I see something different. I see someone slouching to fit into a space smaller than his frame. I see someone who looks small. I wonder about his breathing. I assume, risking projection, that he feels how I felt standing beside that man at the cash register in the Grand Opus. Paralyzed. Breathless. Seething. Restricted. Living in his head and detached from his body.

Why shouldn't he? The NFL owners are his partners, in some ways his peers. Only he and they can truly know the details of their dynamic. But they're all there together in the owner's box, just as I was beside that man in the Grand Opus. Presumably, he and I had paid the same fees to be there. In theory, we had every right to the same space and amenities. But he had more air than I did. He took up my space. I counted down every second until I could get away from him and leave that hotel. Give me a good reason why I should expect Jay-Z to feel any differently sitting there between the owners. *The owners.*

When I look at those images of Jay-Z with NFL commissioner Roger Goodell, or New England Patriots owner Robert Kraft, I don't see the sprawling, dynamic man I met who looked through me with his gaze.

I see myself. Squished between pastel shirts. Snorting at bad jokes. Hoping nobody touches his hair. Gasping for air that money can't buy.

12

The Old Kanye

I guess I should talk about Kanye.

I grew up in a house where my sister and I weren't allowed to use the N-word. We weren't allowed to curse. We were allowed thirty minutes of TV per day, and we weren't allowed to watch music videos or BET at all. My parents, mostly my dad, if I remember correctly, thought that mainstream media's depiction of Black people was lazy, destructive, and undignified.

And yet we were *very much* allowed to listen to hip-hop. Encouraged to do so, even.

When I was almost a teenager, I always enjoyed listening from the hallway when my dad would go into his office, shut the door, and blast Tupac's *All Eyez on Me* album and rap along, making up the words he didn't know here and there. My dad grew up in west Detroit sharing a bed with his brother in the kitchen. He tried to play the part of a middle-class lawyer and father of two artsy, nerdy, privileged Black kids in our suburb of DC—and in many ways, he succeeded—but in that office alone with Tupac, there was a freedom and a defiance in his voice that showed me a side of my dad that I hadn't yet found in myself. I wanted to feel what they felt—the spirit of Tupac and my father—in that room together. Tupac spoke for, and to, Black people who felt wronged and misunderstood and confined by America. He spoke to Black people unwilling to accept a permanent state of victimhood.

As a neighbor to polite white and Asian dentists and doctors and real estate agents and businesspeople, I think my dad needed those moments alone with Tupac to release the parts of himself he tucked into his slacks on the way to parent-teacher conferences at our mostly white middle school. I think Tupac's music gave him space to be completely himself. To hear someone tell the truth.

"You have been wronged. And we're going to make some noise about it. We're gonna make this shit right. You deserve better. I'm here with you." I think that's what Tupac was saying to him.

My dad was born seventeen years before Tupac; I was born seventeen years after. But they shared roots in a dimension of Blackness that I only knew through them. They came from cities, the "inner city" as the cliché goes. Places and times where it was unusual to know Black people with *real* money and options.

Throughout my childhood, my dad would tell me stories of friends who ended up dead, drug addicted, or locked in cages as cautionary tales to keep me focused. They were stories like the ones Tupac told on his albums. Normal people who looked like me and fell to their demise by making mostly rational choices in a lose-lose labyrinth. People who tried to raise their tax bracket and were smacked down by police, judges, neighborhood rivals, and otherwise.

But those stories were just stories to me. I believed them, because they came from voices I trusted—my father, Tupac, Jay-Z, Lil Wayne. But I didn't *know* any real drug dealers. Or gangsters. Or even regular kids who thought there was no way out of the life they had but to take a risk with potentially disastrous consequences. I could feel the music, but I didn't live it.

And then my Tupac emerged.

Drug dealin' just to get by
Stack your money 'til it get sky high
We wasn't s'posed to make it past twenty-five
Joke's on you, we still alive

Those are the first words on the first real track on Kanye's first solo album, *The College Dropout*. I was fifteen years old when it came out. I would turn sixteen three weeks later. Kanye's voice and music soundtracked my coming of age.

I remember driving around in the passenger seat of my dad's MDX SUV truck with my two best friends, Marcus and Justin, both Black like me and also about to turn sixteen, all four of us singing along to each track on the album. Kanye connected my dad—a middle-aged man who came of age in the Detroit riots—with three suburban teenagers who were about to get driver's licenses, lose their virginity, and feel the heavy tension of being Black kids in white neighborhoods.

Kanye was like us. He wore polo shirts and backpacks. He was audacious and insecure. He felt tokenized and marginalized and underpaid at his retail job.

They take me to the back and pat me
Asking me about some khakis
But let some Black people walk in
I bet they show off their token blacky

Kanye was speaking to us. *Us*. By now the Black experience in the inner cities was well-known, although still grossly unremedied. But millions of us were living a more invisible struggle in suburbs where classmates and colleagues assumed we had somehow risen above racism by having houses with garages or yards.

Kanye was talking to us and for us. He wasn't hard. But he was angry. And melodic and vulnerable. He was honest about the fact that he didn't live a criminal life, but he celebrated and loved those who had to live that life to have a chance at another life.

Drug dealin' just to get by
Stack your money 'til it get sky high
We wasn't s'posed to make it past twenty-five
Joke's on you, we still alive

With his lyrics he created a shorthand that helped my dad teach me and my friends, many of whom were growing up without fathers, about what our specific brand of persecution looked like as Black men in America. I could tell it was a joyless duty for my dad to explain to us that we might have to put our hands on the hood of the car and let a police officer aggressively frisk us to stay alive. But Kanye gave us a rhythm for those conversations. He gave us verses to help us first learn the rules of America and then more verses to teach us how to break them.

His artistry was prodigious. He was conflicted. And he spilled his conflicts.

I had a dream I could buy my way to heaven. When I awoke I spent that on a necklace.

He seemed so self-aware about his position as a uniter of Black folks on two different sides of the railroad tracks, but he never felt confined by that position. Kanye's gifts as a musician are singular and undeniable no matter how indefensible he's become. But never mind Kanye's music for just one second.

Kanye was brave. Brave enough to face white people.

George Bush doesn't care about Black people.

I don't think I've lived through a cultural moment that left more of an imprint on me than this one. I was seventeen years old. I had a short Caesar haircut, and I was just about to start my senior year of high school.

I was a ball of hissing, gaslighted code-switching after a decade of being *the Black kid* in most classes and a whole bunch of cars, at house parties, and in student council meetings. I was adept at bending my tone and point of view around white people's feelings, able to challenge them just enough to be heard, but never so bold as to tell the truth.

The whole truth. With my eyes and body. I rarely just said the thing that was always sitting there. If I said it in words, I hid behind a slumped posture or a smirk or a giggle, because to say *the thing* that was honest—"don't say *nigga* around me" or "I'm smarter than you" or "shut the fuck up"—always was to risk gaslighting or alienation or violence.

And then there was Kanye, sitting next to Mike Myers, on the stage at NBCUniversal's *A Concert for Hurricane Relief* broadcast. He stared right down the barrel of the camera and into my gut and changed me forever.

George Bush doesn't care about Black people.

He knew he was right, and he knew it would offend the masses and he didn't fold. He told the truth in front of white people. With his words, with his body, with his gaze, with his voice. He told the truth about white people. I didn't know someone could do that.

I was forever changed. Up to that point, I'd believed the truth was not allowed around white people. A white police officer was never allowed to know that I knew my rights and that I knew I was supposed to have the same rights as everyone else. My white teachers were not allowed to know that I knew I was smarter than my classmates and that my parents were better educated than they were. My white classmates were not allowed to know that I didn't like the movies they liked, that their jokes weren't funny, and that the *real* reason they weren't allowed to come over to hang at my house is because we didn't trust them.

America had taught me by way of Emmett Till and Rosa Parks and every moment in between that to look whiteness in the eye and tell the truth was a highly punishable offense. It was just not allowed.

As far as I could tell, white people got to live in a house of mirrors that always reflected back to them a smile and a lie more palatable than the truth that they were the cause of incredible pain and suffering. For a moment, on national television, Kanye shattered those mirrors. How brave.

And he was just so—*normal.* He was up there on that set, with his very average build, wearing a polo like the ones me and my friends wore to the teen clubs in Rockville. He said the thing. He was just a year into his solo career as an artist. And he did it. He said the truth, despite white people. He risked everything in that moment.

In doing so he showed me how potent the truth could be. I would eventually learn that telling the truth that way, exactly as one sees it, is *that thing* that makes a writer. That's the ever voice for which we all strive. He had it, and he wielded it with the highest stakes. I'm sure he didn't mean to, but he gave me, and people like me, a gift at that moment. I saw what it takes for a voice to cut through.

When I think and write bravely as Kanye did in that moment, I have a chance to make something meaningful. When I bend my body and point of view around people's demands and insecurities like I did for my white friends as a teenager, I don't even have a shot. Now, every time I sit in front of a microphone or a keyboard, I seek to create something with that sort of potent honesty. That sort of truth is scarce, which is what makes it valuable. In the times when I can tap into it, I can sell my voice and my writing and use that to feed me. In the times when I'm too afraid, I try to think back to Kanye in his twenties and how he showed me what it means to be vulnerable and brave at the same time.

I'm not sure what to make of what Kanye's become in his middle age, spouting off Nazi rhetoric and wearing White Lives Matter shirts. I know that it's scary because he once seemed to me like someone who knew how to move toward freedom. He seemed to have a compass that pointed toward confidence and liberation. And his musical gifts made it so enticing to follow him in that direction. But now he seems lost, which is worrisome, because I spent so many years following him. Does that mean I too am lost? I don't think so, but the idea makes me think it's unsafe to follow anyone if someone who once felt so grounded and unafraid can turn out to be so misguided and seemingly fearful.

As a response to watching people like Kanye lose their way, I've decided not to follow anyone. In my career I've rejected being a part of any particular producer or artist's loyal camp. Each super-creative in Hollywood has their own fiefdom. Steven Spielberg has his. Spike Lee has his. Kenya Barris, Issa Rae, Donald Glover . . . Each has their own, and the list goes on. For a brief time, I thought I'd be part of Spike Lee's camp, and then Kanye's thereafter. But I never stick because I can't help but think that if I'm underwritten by someone else, then that means they're taking home the lion's share of the money and glory that we collectively create. I don't blame them for that; that's just how things work. As a result, I always feel like a loner in the abyss in this industry. But that's better than feeling like a follower. Looking out into space without a map or someone else's footprints to guide me is a form of freedom that I cherish most.

Once, however, I was very close to being a part of Kanye West's camp. He had been my favorite artist for fifteen years at that point, and I got to witness his potent honesty up close. We were connected by a TV producer with whom we both worked closely. He brought me into Kanye's world to hang out sometimes, play basketball, go to the movies, and once we even visited the West-Kardashian household in Calabasas. Our colleague's intent was to spark a creative connection between us so I might help Kanye continue to build his empire. Presumably, I'd be paid in some way for this work, but I can't say we ever reached that point. This was all before Kanye's public meltdown, and as a writer with few credits to my name, I was ecstatic to have the opportunity.

We started one of our days working together at Kanye's Yeezy Studio in Calabasas. This was out in the desert, about forty-five minutes outside LA. The outside of the offices was nondescript and looked much like the outside of any other boring corporate office anywhere in America. But inside, the space was designed with a tasteful, minimalist approach: off-white studio space scattered with clothing material samples, drawings, and floor designs. There, I was among a few dozen creatives who were each contributing in their own disciplines to the creative projects at hand. Most of the other creatives looked like they were in a similar position to mine—young, hungry, and trying not to look surprised by their amazing fortune to be working with Kanye West. I signed an NDA, so I can't and won't describe any of the projects in detail, but I have felt tickled each time I've seen some animated advertisement or shoe released to the public that I first saw in its early stages in that studio.

To my eye Kanye showed no signs of the white supremacy and anti-Semitism he'd be spewing just a few years later. In fact, he came off as warm but a little shy, friendly, silly, and somewhat immature in his humor. His inner child was present always and most apparent in how purely he followed his impulses throughout the day.

One moment we were eating brunch while he scrolled through Instagram showing us photos of people he knew and telling us what they were like. In an instant, he was ready to leave, the bill was paid by one of his friends (or something), and we were off to follow his next desire. On the way to the car, a paparazzo jumped out in the parking lot and snapped photos of Kanye while we walked. He giggled and ducked his head down. It occurs to me now that I was entourage.

We were driving toward Hollywood, heading to a movie theater, when Kanye was struck by a new idea. It was time to work on something creative.

So the three of us—Kanye, our colleague, and me—drove up the 101 highway. Our colleague drove and Kanye sat in the passenger seat staring out the window taking in the beautiful coastal scenery, bobbing to his own music. I sat in the middle seat in the back.

Our colleague asked for the name of my favorite Kanye song—"Runaway." He turned it on the car speakers as loud as possible and we listened and sang along. When the song concluded, it was time to work.

I opened a notebook that's sitting in a drawer next to me in my office now. The producer informed me that my role for the day was notetaker. So, I came prepared with a list of questions and ideas and a sequence in mind as to how our creative discussion would go should we ever get to it. I was excited for my chance to show value that way.

Kanye riffed as we drove, excavating his mind for enormous ideas for music, movies, TV, live installations, every form of art and entertainment. He spewed a complex web of concepts and producers and directors that was difficult to follow. I tried. I wrote furiously into my journal, trying to capture each thought while he moved quickly on to the next.

I lost my grip on the conversation in one of his transitions and felt I needed to regain my footing or else fail in my job as notetaker. I interjected and asked him to return to his previous train of thought.

The car went silent. I saw our colleague do a half grimace, half smile in the rearview mirror. He knew where this was headed.

Kanye chortled for just a second. But this wasn't a childlike laugh or a silly one. It was a scoff.

He looked back at me, through me. Straight into my eyeballs. His face straightened out and became serious.

"You running the meeting now?" he said.

Those words shot down my spine, and I felt all the blood rush out of my feet. My face tightened. I tried to look serious and dignified, but I felt like my head was going to explode. I thought he was going to press an eject button that would spring me through the sunroof and shoot me straight back to Bed-Stuy.

Kanye didn't eject me, but just that quickly he made sure I knew not to speak out of turn for the rest of our session.

I had broken a golden rule of creativity: Never interrupt an artist in flow.

His reaction stung me. I had come so far on this journey, to the point that I was sitting right next to—well, behind—one of my creative idols. But I spoke out of turn, and his response made me feel like I'd just ripped off a loud fart in algebra class.

I was shell-shocked for the next ten minutes, but he quickly regained footing and continued down his creative path while I took notes as best I could.

And I left that moment with two important lessons.

The first: It's an artistic crime to try to force a creative path. I may have blocked the way to an amazing breakthrough by disrupting the flow to stick to some script in my notebook that I had made up. I was anxious about not understanding Kanye's process, and that led me to ambush his creative space. I now try to avoid doing that to others, and I get very impatient when people do it to me. That was my last creative session with Kanye. Just a few months later, Kanye famously said "Slavery was a choice" in an interview with TMZ, and soon thereafter I lost touch with the friend who once connected us.

My second takeaway from that moment regards the value of honesty. Honesty is often thought of as the truth in words. But there's more to it. Honesty is tonal. Honesty is about the speed between impulse and action. I think most people in Kanye's shoes at that moment would have found some halfway to communicate that I had disrupted their process. Maybe they would have winced instead of making eye contact and obliged me a full thirty seconds to steer us down a path they didn't believe in to avoid confrontation. They would have squirmed or seethed while waiting for me to shut up. The funk would have lingered well past the moment.

Maybe they would have wrapped their whole being around a lie and pretended to follow me down the path I wanted to follow so that I could feel more a part of the process. That would have confused me. I would have lost sight of my true role as notetaker in a way that would distort my value and compromise the mission. We would have become three people on an unclear path steered by whoever spoke last.

But instead, this very complicated figure opted in that moment for honesty. He was mad and needed me to get with the program. And he communicated that with his voice, his body, his eye contact, his entire being. And from there, he returned to the mission, clear and aligned. And I followed, stung but in order.

The value of honesty is that it moves in straight lines. It repairs misalignment. After that moment I understood my role in the process and much more about the creative process at large. It hurts now to see what Kanye is becoming, because he gave me that incredible gift.

I have observed that same sort of radical candor in other impactful artists. They are honest and they are wealthy. I could shoehorn a connection between those traits, but I'm not sure which is chicken and which is egg.

Honesty is powerful, and I believe it leads to deeper understanding between people in creative partnerships, which often results in better art. But money is also powerful. Maybe it offers a person more space, more confidence, more authority to speak from the gut. Would I have been so honest with Kanye had he interrupted my train of thought? Of course not. Not then. Today? Maybe. But only because he and others showed me the value of honesty.

13

Directed by Spike Lee

These days, Spike Lee is a distant mentor who checks in twice a year or so to show support for a project, catch up for lunch, or talk through creative ideas. But Spike was someone I talked to daily when I was first entering the entertainment industry. He was a godfather of sorts who walked me past the gatekeepers.

I don't know a more honest communicator. When I'd share a script idea with Spike, he would stare at me through his red, thick-rimmed glasses, showing no emotion. When I reached the big climax moment his entire body would explode in reaction. In the best moments, he'd unfurl a big smile, throw his head back, and laugh out loud.

"FREAKY DEAKY!" he'd yell in the middle of the crowded Academy Restaurant in Fort Greene.

In the worst moments, I'd hit the punchline of my spiel and his body would give. His shoulders would slouch, and he'd crouch down into pitiful disappointment.

"Whoa! No. I don't think you want to say that, my brother," he'd say. This was a more loving and kind way of offering critical feedback than Kanye's. Granted, Spike is older, wiser, and had a deeper connection to me than Kanye, who likely saw me as one of hundreds of mercenary creatives floating around in his orbit.

But Spike's honesty encouraged me to go back to the lab, determined to return with something that would impress him.

In either moment there was nothing left to interpret. Spike's speed between impulse and action was instantaneous. Spike let his whole spirit show what he felt. Unfettered. Unblocked. Even in a room full of people.

That is freedom. Honesty is freedom.

There were many times when Spike's honesty hit me in a way that stuck. He was always trying to save time. Small talk was unallowed. There were big ideas to tend to and no time to chew on trivialities.

But still, he was (and remains) a legend to me, so I felt a duty to lead each interaction with deference and pleasantries. I'd always try to start a conversation by asking him about something human—how was his day going? How was his family?

Those are polite things to ask someone, but in truth, I didn't care that much. I knew the urgent matter was the TV series we were developing together. We needed to work so that we could sell it to a network and make some money. So he could continue building his artistic empire and I could pay my bills. So all my well-meaning pleasantries were dishonest. He cut right through them one day.

I'd called Spike to ask him a few questions about an upcoming trip to LA. Even though we'd been working together for a couple months at that point, I was still awed each time I tapped Spike Lee's name on the cracked screen of my iPhone and *the* Spike Lee answered on the other end. So I led nervously with those pleasantries to give myself a chance to gain some composure.

"Hello," he said.

"Hi, Spike. Um. Hi, it's Chad. How are you?"

"Good," he said.

"Oh. Um, well. How's your day going? Are you doing all right?"

"I'm good," he replied.

"Well, okay. I know you are probably very busy. So, anyway. Um, so is now a good time?"

I was stumbling. He'd had enough.

"Chad. My Morehouse brother. Just talk," he directed.

He went silent and waited. Understanding washed over me. I realized that when two people are connected, pleasantries are a distraction. They're an offense, even.

We both knew what we were here for. We knew the mission. And I understood his silence shouldn't make me uncomfortable. His silence meant he was listening. It was up to me to fill the silence with honesty. I should have done the work of knowing what I had to say before calling.

From there, we had a direct and productive conversation. Spike had given me permission to get straight to the point. He required it. Our conversations changed after that. I relaxed in them. I came to each conversation with my thoughts composed, which made it easier to exchange new thoughts on impulse.

Spike gave me permission to just talk. I didn't need to fill each sentence or paragraph with packaging. It was my right to just say exactly what I needed to say. My thoughts began to flow more freely from source to message. I was unstuck.

14

"You're Not Rich."

Money is so pungent that even little kids are aware of who has it and who is supposed to have it. Children learn early on how to detect and leverage this power. I first recognized this truth when I was around eleven years old, attending a birthday party for my godfather's son who was also my cousin-in-law. The Birthday Boy lived in a wealthy part of New Jersey where his Black family owned two very large houses conjoined by a giant backyard in a predominantly white neighborhood.

His father—my godfather—was a hardworking, successful lawyer known for his enormous laugh and gregarious personality.

This birthday party, held in the lavish, conjoined backyard, was attended by dozens of family friends, work friends, hired clowns, ventriloquists, animals for petting, balloon modelers, and even a caricature artist who drew cartoon portraits of my family members that still sit framed in my parents' living room. The Birthday Boy was turning nine, and he had many rounds to make among the hundred-plus guests frolicking in his double-backyard. But at some point, the Birthday Boy, my thirteen-year-old sister, our six-year-old cousin, and I found ourselves together on the blacktop playing with chalk. There were a couple other kids within earshot, forming a loose, momentary play tribe as kiddies do.

Birthday Boy shot a question into the air apropos of nothing.

"Is anyone else here rich?"

My sister and I waited in earnest for anyone to respond. We weren't rich, but we could feel that we were among at least a few other rich people, and I was interested in seeing them reveal themselves.

"I'm rich," our six-year-old cousin responded in a sweet, tentative, rug rat voice.

"I've been to your house. You're not rich," said Birthday Boy dismissively. The Birthday Boy scooped up his piece of chalk and walked away unceremoniously.

In that moment, I learned that our cousin wasn't rich, and I think she did too. I watched her for a beat. I was worried she might cry. She stood there processing with a blank look on her face. I've seen that same look on the faces of toddlers when they fall on the floor and search the room for adult cues to tell them whether to cry or not.

In the years since, my sister and I have repeated the line to each other again and again: "I've been to your house. You're not rich."

What sticks in my mind is that he had already sized up our cousin's family and their money situation. Either that, or he'd overheard other adult family members doing it aloud. He knew before she spoke up that our cousin wasn't rich—at least not in his eyes. Imagine five people in your life, the first five who come to mind. I bet just as easily as you can see their faces in your mind, you can put a dollar sign next to each face that accounts to how much money you think they have.

And if you can't, it's because you've tried to and couldn't come up with a number.

Birthday Boy didn't have to measure up our cousin right then and there on the blacktop. His question was rhetorical; he already knew her answer, just as he knew mine and my sister's. He had assigned her a value: not rich. We all do that. We estimate what someone is worth and treat them accordingly. Money and race are inextricably linked in that valuation process. And the process begins as soon as a person has consciousness and continues until death.

UCLA developmental psychologist Dr. Rashmita Mistry's research shows that children as young as five years old have keen economic awareness. Children know that rich people get to live a certain way, that people in the middle classes live differently, and that people in poverty live differently altogether. Likewise, children understand that white people have access to a certain lifestyle, that non-white people have access to another lifestyle, and that Black people live a separate lifestyle altogether. Children are observant. Those are the rules, and in most cases they hold. When those rules appear to have been bent or broken, they notice.

But it can take many people a lifetime to understand or accept that those rules were designed to keep certain people on the bottom so that others can live on their backs. It took me until my late twenties to *truly* start to question and understand the intentional design of class and race and their intersection. It was more soothing to look away.

The intentional design built to keep Black people on the bottom of both racial and financial hierarchies is described and interrogated by Isabel Wilkerson in her masterpiece *Caste*, which sits behind me at the top of my bookshelf so I never forget what great writing looks like.

I was reading a hardcover copy of *Caste* on my way from New

York to Los Angeles sitting, for the first time in my life, in first-class seats that I had paid for with my own money. I splurged because I was celebrating my trip to go shoot the first few episodes of my podcast, *Quitters*, with my co-host, Julie Bowen. There was a little white girl no older than twelve sitting in the seat behind mine with her mother and a friend of the girl's age. They were sitting in the section just between first class and economy, the "extra room" area. As we flew, I heard the girl complain to her mother several times about the lack of space and ask why they weren't seated in first class as usual. The mother apologized in whispers to her daughter for their seating and assured her she'd be more comfortable on the next flight. The little girl questioned her mother aloud throughout the flight, talking over her, interrupting her, and demanding more snacks and entertainment options that weren't available on Delta Air Lines.

The girl's voice was a distraction from my reading at times, but none of it shocked me. I've seen rich white kids talk to their parents before.

But just before we started our initial descent into LA, something she said did shock me.

Like the Birthday Boy, this little girl shot out an observation unrelated to any conversation going on.

"All white people are upper class, and all dark people are lower class. Mom, will we be at the front of the plane for the next flight?"

She was underscoring the real question she'd been asking her mom the entire time. *We're white. Why are we sitting back here when there are dark people sitting in first class?*

The little girl's mom tried to shush her, but she didn't tell her she was wrong. It was an apt observation. What in the world was she doing back there with me sitting up here? Kids know the rules.

I took note of the section of *Caste* that I was reading when I heard the little girl speak up. I couldn't believe the irony.

> *In America, the South Carolina Negro Code of 1735 went so far as to specify the fabrics enslaved black people were permitted to wear, forbidding any that might be seen as above their station. They were banned from wearing, "any sort of garment or apparel whatsoever, finer, other or of greater value than Negro cloth, duffels, coarse kerseys, osnaburg, blue linen, check linen, or coarse garlix, or calicoes," the cheapest, roughest fabrics available to the colony. Two hundred years later, the spirit of the law was still in force as African American soldiers were set upon and killed for wearing their army uniforms.*

Rules like these remain upheld today. Black people are expected to be poor, and if we're not, we're at least expected to appear to be so for the comfort of white people. My sitting in first class upset this little girl. I believe her response to my seating was a reflex. She saw something that didn't make sense: myself and others who looked like me having access that she didn't. It made her feel bad. Maybe it made *her* feel dark. She complained aloud and her mother didn't correct her. Maybe she thought that what her daughter was pointing out was indeed an injustice and that we should have switched seats. In any case, I should be punished for the mis-seating by having to be reminded that usually this is not how we would be arranged. The rules are that that little white girl should never have to feel like I have something that she can't have.

That's why the code Wilkerson outlined is so important. The words change over time, and sometimes they're altogether lifted from the policies and codes that govern our country, but they're upheld just the same. If I sit in first class, I'll be punished by observation. If I wear jewelry or clothes too expensive or drive a car too flashy, I may attract the attention and ire of police. Because that's the code. Whites in front, Blacks in the back. I must not wear any garment or apparel of greater value than Negro cloth. But those types of garments and seating arrangements and cars and so many other forbidden things are the signals of wealth. They, along with my Black skin, tell people how to treat me. Even kids recognize their implications. So without them, I'm ushered along to the back and dismissed.

You're not rich. I've seen your house.

That's the code. It's confining. It incites me to be defiant. Sometimes I wear a big, shiny, fake gold chain with a shiny black medallion in it. I like how it draws attention. I like how it makes people wonder how to place me. But before I leave the house with it on, my then fiancée reminds me to tuck it in my shirt while I'm in the car for my safety. Otherwise I might attract the wrong attention from those who don't want to see me appearing *above my station.*

15

Jack and Jill and the Black Elite

I've been doing the awkward dance of trying to signal that I have enough money to be valued but not so much that I'm unrelatable since high school. That's when I felt my peers fervently dialing in their assumptions about me using whatever clues they had. Signs of money and wealth are so often the default identifiers when we're sizing each other up, and in my observation, no one is more readily coiled to accept or cast off another than the anxious, unsettled teen.

When I was sixteen years old my girlfriend at the time, Zoe, offered me a ride home after a high school football game. A tall, easy-going guy named Daron who played on her school's basketball team had already jumped in the back seat of her car to tag along for the ride. They were close friends who lived in the same neighborhood ten minutes from my house. I paused for a beat before accepting Zoe's offer. Daron had never been to my house. I was self-conscious about what Daron would think of me when he saw that we lived in a single-family home on a cul-de-sac, with a two-car garage, and a well-kept, lush green lawn. I was quiet during the ride over as my girlfriend and Daron joked around and rapped along to "Lost Ones" by Lauryn Hill, which was playing on WPGC 95.5 FM.

It's funny how money change a situation.

Miscommunication lead to complication.

I was silent, calculating how I would defend myself when Daron went back and told the other kids at Zoe's school that I was living much more comfortably than most Black kids in our county.

As we pulled into my neighborhood full of large, single-family homes with spacious lawns and backyards and tall trees, the energy in the car shifted. Zoe turned down the radio as I'd asked her to do when driving down those streets. Daron was quiet now too. I watched him through the rearview mirror as he took in the houses, their lawn-scapes and garages, and the German shepherds and Doberman pinschers guarding them, prowling around inside brown-and-white gates. Zoe rolled to a stop in front of our house and Daron broke the silence.

"Damn, Chad's people living good out here," he joked.

Daron laughed. I forcibly laughed. Zoe didn't. She knew I was embarrassed. I kissed Zoe on the cheek and dapped up Daron and went inside—by myself. I didn't invite them in because it was enough for Daron to know what the outside of our house looked like. I didn't want him to come in and see the baby grand piano in the family room, or photos of my cousin Trooper standing in the White House beside President Clinton, with whom he worked closely for many years. I didn't want Daron to notice the full bookshelves in each room. By now I knew this was unusual to some people because every friend who came to our house mentioned how many books we had. I didn't want Daron to know that the refrigerator and pantry were full of food, so full that my dad put another refrigerator in the garage to hold the surplus. I didn't want him to know that my parents had the kitchen remodeled just for a change or that there were big flat-screen TVs in the living room and lower level of the house when big flat-screen TVs were still a rarity.

I didn't want Daron to know anything else about me, about us, because what he saw from the driveway was enough. He had already sized me up, right there in the driveway. I could tell by his tone. *Chad's people living good.*

He had taken a note to self. I was one of *them.*

He now saw me as different from him, and from Zoe for that matter, because from what he could see my family had money. Now I was on the other side of the line from them. And I wasn't about to make the gap between us any wider by inviting him into the house so he could see exactly how far apart we stood.

Daron and Zoe drove off, and I went inside and lived in my head for the rest of the night regretting that I'd let Daron get that close. I've lived my entire life, since childhood, with an insecurity around being Black and upper middle class. I'd already felt many times what I perceived to be judgment from other Black folks for not embodying the *entire* struggle; that my upper middle classness somehow watered down my Black experience. As a teenaged ball of frayed nerves and sensitivity, I couldn't talk myself down from the shame I felt about my family's comfortable lifestyle under Daron's gaze.

I saw Daron many times after that interaction because he was a close friend of Zoe's, but we never recovered from that moment. Each time I saw him, I felt his distance, his refusal to make eye contact, a change in his tone between how he talked to other kids and how he talked to me. He almost mocked how I spoke by faux-matching me with his own voice. He talked to me like a whitewashed nerd, like Carlton Banks. Over time, his friends joined in on the mocking. They might not have even known *why* he was mocking me, but teenagers are impressionable. The mocking was often subtle, but it was there. Daron and I shared another close friend who I'm still close with today. He confirmed for me many years later that they saw me as an outsider and that Daron reported back to the group that we had a *huge house living by them white folks.*

They pieced a story together about what I was. To them, I was one of *those* Black people. A Black elitist. A Jack and Jill kid. Their behavior toward me was a direct response to feeling looked down upon by other Black people in our community who behaved as though they were better than the rest of us. And as much as I resented those kids for seeing me that way, I related to their feelings then, and I still do.

That day with Daron and Zoe came during my junior year of high school. A couple years after that, I made my first effort to escape the vicious judgment and competition endemic to what I'll call the Black elite circles of the Washington, DC, metro area. My childhood was a process of urgently trying to endear myself to many different types of people. My parents were young, Black professionals: my dad a lawyer, my mom a corporate executive at Verizon (then Bell Atlantic). In their early thirties, they moved from Washington, DC, to Montgomery County, Maryland, to raise me and my sister somewhere with a bit more space to run around. Today, I'm watching my sister and her husband raise their three boys while I mentally prepare for fatherhood myself one day. I'm floored by the exhausting mental gymnastics Black parents go through trying to find communities for their children where they can be safe and nurtured without pulling them away from Black communities.

For my parents, that calculus resulted in countless school visits to determine where to send my sister and me almost every year from pre-K all the way to high school. My parents would go to prospective schools and sit through classes to see if the teachers were addressing the Black kids directly or ignoring them and letting them sit in the back of the class and tune out. They had to see if the Black kids were elevating, getting the same opportunities as other kids, getting good grades, getting into college. My parents were tirelessly focused on making sure me and my sister got what they deemed to be the best opportunities in school. That meant moving me from school to school almost every other year, tracking the very white and Asian gifted and talented public school programs in our county. As a result, I went to three different elementary schools, two middle schools, and two high schools. All the while my parents kept me involved in basketball teams, a Black Cub Scout troop, church programs, bands, and—that's right—*Jack and Jill*, to keep me close to other Black kids.

By jumping from environment to environment so often, I learned how to assess hierarchies quickly.

As my young brain developed, observations fermented. *At this school the Black kids love basketball and the white kids love Pokémon.* Then I'd set to work getting better at basketball and begging my parents to buy me overpriced Pokémon cards so I could endear myself to both groups. I had to move quickly if I wanted to fit in. I felt this urgent rush to not always be the loner new kid. I felt that primal, tribal push to find a clique.

Once I'd spent many years in the "gifted and talented" classrooms with the white kids, it became more difficult for me to get the Black kids to love me. I think they saw my inclusion in the white classrooms as a betrayal. Even then, we knew that the "gifted and talented" classes had the best teachers and classroom resources. We had state-of-the-art computers and brand-new textbooks each year, as compared to the old, hand-me-down materials in the general population classes. The public school system made it clear early on that white and Asian kids deserved better than the rest of us. And because I was inside those primarily white classrooms, I think my Black schoolmates probably saw me as a traitor, or someone who was willing to leave them behind for better access. In that way, they may have felt their own tribalism kick in, an unconscious voice telling them that *I* was the one who was outcasting *them*.

In seventh grade, my middle school girlfriend was a very pretty Black girl named Laynee whose parents were Ethiopian immigrants. I remember thinking she was so special for overlooking the fact that I was the kid in all the white classes, for still seeing me as dateable. But shortly after we got together, a few of the Black boys in our school began to threaten me and intimidate me. They'd catch me in the corners of the hallways between classes and tell me they were going to fight me if I hung around too long after school. They were bigger than me as most boys my age were, and they wore the clothes my parents wouldn't let me spend money on—North Face jackets and Jordan sneakers and François Girbaud jeans. These were the kids I wanted most to like me, to love me. They were the cool Black kids, the ones who seemed most edgy and most masculine. And not only did they not like me, they wanted to hurt me. I can't say they didn't love me, though, because maybe their anger toward me was their way of expressing a poisoned love.

After all, I was supposed to be one of them. I looked like them despite our fashion differences. But I had committed one of the great violations. They didn't say so exactly, but I knew they were mad that I had crossed over the line and then doubled back to date a Black girl. My first violation was to be the Black kid in the classes with the white kids and the fancy computers. Now I had the nerve to reach back across the line to date one of the Black girls. I was as surprised as they were that she was interested in me, but it made them boil with pubescent, testosterone-fueled rage. Laynee was unaffected by the entire thing, but it consumed me. I felt like I was in real danger. Maybe I was.

Each time I ran into a couple of these boys in the emptier hallways or stairwells they'd buck at me like they were going to hit me and then pull back their fists at the last second. They'd make throat slashing gestures at me in front of Laynee, or they'd just flat-out yell at me from across the hall.

"I'm gonna fuck you up, Chad!"

Middle schoolers aren't creative with their threats. And they always included my name each time they threatened me. Sometimes they were smiling. There was a high level of intimacy in this cat and mouse game.

They bullied me constantly for the first half of that year, and I was scared. I had never been in a real fight, and I had no Black friends at the school to stand with me. None of the white kids from my classes offered to help, and I'm pretty sure none even noticed what I was going through. Thinking back on it, it's incredible how oblivious the white kids at school were to what I was experiencing. Even as preteens, white people live heedless of the terrors of Black people in their lives.

Once I was sure that these kids were going to hurt me, I woke up each day dreading the car ride to school. When I couldn't take the anxiety anymore, I finally told my mom enough to try to get myself out of going to school altogether. One Monday my mom pulled up our Volvo in front of Colonel E. Brooke Lee Middle School, and I just started crying. I told her that the Black kids at school didn't accept me, that I was so sad and scared to have to go to school that day.

My mom was heartbroken, but of course I had to go to school. The kids didn't hurt me that day, but their threats continued. That night at the dinner table, my mom and I talked to my dad about what was going on. My dad assured both of us that when basketball season started, I would make the team and the Black kids would come around to me. Day after day, the threats continued to the point where I got used to them; eventually I could even ignore them. Laynee and I drifted apart without so much as a conversation, as preteen romances go. And then basketball season came around. Lo and behold, my dad was right. My status turned. The Black boys admired me because I could hoop. Basketball was my saving grace for the rest of middle and high school. It was my way of showing the Black kids that I hadn't crossed over just because I was in the other classes. It saved me.

But that day in the car with my mom had a lasting impact on both of us. My mom could see that I was growing into adolescence and the threats of violence and other problems were becoming more real for her Black son. (That threat of violence would remain in my life to this day, as I've shared in these pages.)

My mom foresaw these potential dangers looming for her Black babies many years before they actually closed in on me as a teenager. She knew that entering us in the gifted and talented track in the public schools would mean my sister and I would both be isolated as Black kids in mostly white classrooms, with many other Black students at our schools who *weren't* in those classes seeing us as different from them. Early in my childhood, my mom did what she thought was best to protect us from that confusing, isolating circumstance: When I was in elementary school, she applied and was accepted into Jack and Jill of America, Inc., an organization for Black mothers and their families whose website boasts "262 chapters nationwide, representing more than 50,000 family members. Each chapter plans annual programming activities guided under a general five point programmatic thrust: cultural awareness, educational development, health (education and advocacy), civic (legislative advocacy and service) and social/recreational areas." The organization was originally formed during the Great Depression by Black mothers with the intention of bringing kids together in social and cultural settings.

My opinion of this organization was formed first as a kid who was a member from ages nine to eighteen. Then, I loved having a place to go to hang out with other Black kids who didn't ostracize me the way the other Black kids at school did—at least until basketball saved me. But even then, as a preteen, I noticed how this organization separated Black families from one another, and sometimes even forced divisions within Black families.

It has always been difficult for families to gain acceptance into Jack and Jill. The Jack and Jill membership website reads, "prospective members must be sponsored by a current member in good standing of the chapter in which they are seeking membership. We encourage interested mothers to make contact with Jack and Jill members in their local communities to learn about specific membership guidelines and procedures. If you are unfamiliar with any current members of your local chapter, you may choose to network with others in your community to gain contact with a chapter member. Please be aware that membership intake is at the sole discretion of each chapter. Obtaining a sponsor does not guarantee intake into the organization."

In so many words, Jack and Jill is a members' club for Black families, and it was the first of several exclusive clubs for Black people to which I have belonged. I went to a college—Morehouse—known for being one of the top HBCUs. As an entering freshman, I applied to be accepted into its most exclusive dormitory—Graves Hall, the campus's oldest building. Seeking greater elite status, in my sophomore year I joined the Morehouse chapter of the Alpha Phi Alpha Fraternity, Inc. Alpha was the first and oldest of the Divine Nine Black fraternities and sororities, and our chapter, Alpha Rho, was known to be the most exclusive within the fraternity. After college, once I moved into the entertainment industry, I became a part of a small group of Black creatives in entertainment seeking equity in the industry.

Each of these schools, organizations, and clubs comprise communities built around important missions to elevate Black people, but each is rife with hierarchy and an air of status that make them alluring, competitive, and exhausting all at once. And to some Black people who aren't welcome, they can be marginalizing. But I first became familiar with, if not indoctrinated by, these sorts of exclusive organizations for Black people in my childhood as a member of Jack and Jill. And that's when I first began to understand the divides these sorts of organizations can cause between us.

As a kid, I noticed my friends from church and Cub Scouts and basketball make snide comments about my family for being part of Jack and Jill. They complained that members—like us—thought they were better than other Black people. They would raise their pinkies in the air and imitate me and my family having fancy dinners together. They would insult us and say that we had done favors and chores for other Black families to gain admittance. And, of course, they would say we never would have gotten into the organization if we didn't have money.

The virulence of their sentiments confused me. As an adult, I realize that their parents must have been sharing these feelings with them in private or in ways I couldn't detect as a child. Because I was a member, I could see that most of Jack and Jill's activities consisted of innocuous things like laser tag and teen dances, Thanksgiving dinners for the families, community celebrations, and the occasional co-ed sleepover for the kids. But I didn't realize that drawing a line around this circle of insiders emitted a signal of elitism and separatism to other Black families, especially those who tried to enter and were rejected. A friend of mine from college jokes that his mother wasn't accepted into the organization because his family wasn't fancy enough. Still, he says, he'll try to have his own family accepted when he has kids because of the value of the network. But he's the most diplomatic of Black folks I know when it comes to opinions on this community.

On a recent Fourth of July weekend, I was part of a loud, heated conversation among friends about the organization. It was late at night, on the shore of Inkwell Beach at Martha's Vineyard, a vacation destination famously frequented by Jack and Jill–ers and others who many would describe as members of the Black elite. One friend, who did not grow up in such circles, argued loudly that Jack and Jill was poison to the Black community because it made certain young Black people feel at an early age that they were better than their peers. He observed that those elitist young people then clung to that status as their entire identity throughout their lives, at the expense of other Black people—and even themselves. He pointed to me and other friends of ours from college as examples of people he knew, and loved, who lived with a sense of entitlement because we came from Jack and Jill families with money. I thought about a time when we were driving around in Atlanta in an Acura he'd saved up to buy. I spilled soda all over his seats. He was so angry at me, and my response to him was, "Bruh, it's just an Acura." I imagine he endured and witnessed many moments like that around the large contingent of Jack and Jill kids and Black elitists at our college.

I had no real counterargument against his point of view on the organization and Black elitism at large. I said that organizations like Jack and Jill exist to offer Black families the support of a strong network, which is valuable because we are up against so much anti-Blackness in the workplace and in schools and in society. But my voice wasn't strong. My argument boiled down to the idea that Black people in this organization find strength by isolating ourselves and rejecting the larger community. That makes no sense, and I knew it then. But still, I had grown up in this institution, and I felt compelled to defend its existence, however feebly.

I found myself again having to weigh my impulse to defend Jack and Jill and the self-proclaimed Black "elite" while at work last year.

I was one of HBO Max's twelve writers for the first season of the series *Rap Sh!t*. The writers' room, which existed entirely on Zoom, was staffed almost entirely by Black writers—mostly women—and zero white guys. That makeup offered a space for honest conversation to explore gender, race, class, sex, ego, greed, family, and many other topics without fear of being trampled by *The Man* or having to tiptoe around his sensitivities. But a conversation arose surrounding Jack and Jill and the Black elite that bumped against *my* sensitivities. Suddenly, *I* was sitting in the seat as *The Man.*

As was common, our conversation had veered away from the characters in our series and into our own lives and Black culture. This sort of detour was how we excavated storylines that felt honest. One of my colleagues was revving up her opinions about Black elitism and Jack and Jill. I braced myself because TV writers can be especially knifing with words. Many of us, myself included, use the page as a place to purge our most incendiary thoughts and feelings, those not suited for casual conversation. This colleague was the most searing among us, and I could feel in her tone that there would be casualties in this conversation. I hoped not to catch a stray.

She remarked at the stupidity and self-hate in Black people looking down at other Black people because one group has money and a sort of fake, insider status that the other doesn't. She quipped that those elitist communities were anti-Black themselves, and that the members wanted so badly to be white that they tried to separate themselves from their own people. Other Black writers in the room cosigned her diatribe, laughing and joking and taking their own stabs at Jack and Jill–ers and Black elitists. We as a writers' room chose a different societal element as a piñata each day, taking turns swinging our bats against it until it burst open and we all laughed before getting back to work. It was tribal. It was a mental vacation from the strenuous work of writing the first season of a highly anticipated TV series, Issa Rae's follow-up to *Insecure*, the show that elevated Issa to first name only creator status in Hollywood and was finishing out its final season.

Though it was never made explicit, we all felt the pressure to follow *Insecure* with a product that held up to its predecessor *and* carved enough of its own path to discourage constant comparisons. First seasons are the most difficult to concoct, and our success or failure would likely determine whether or not HBO Max commissioned a second season. The pressure of our mandate combined with the maddening strain of staring at little Zoom boxes on our computers for five hours at a time meant that we needed these little piñata-whacking sessions to unite us and give us a release. But this time I felt like *I* was the piñata, and each swing of the bat made me more nauseous. I was stewing silently under each insult to the Jack-and-Jill type.

Self-hating.

Uncle Toms.

Brown paper bag–testers.

I tried to look like I was having a good time in case anyone was clocking me in my Zoom box, but I didn't throw any insults of my own into the fray. I just chuckled along awkwardly. *And I would have gotten away with it too* but there was another writer on the show who I'd known since childhood. She was the same person who had dropped me off at my parents' house in high school, with Daron in the back seat, who outed me as upper middle class to the other Black kids at their school. She and I also went to college together. She knew exactly how I'd grown up. She knew I'd been in Jack and Jill for most of my childhood. She knew my money and status consciousness. She knew I was insecure about how much I clocked money and status, and how much I cared to fill myself up with both. She didn't out me, but I'm sure she saw me there, hiding as an imposter, just trying to let the moment pass. I didn't like that feeling. I didn't like knowing that one of the eleven people in the "room" knew I was pretending to be someone I wasn't, or pretending to *not* be someone I was. When I feel squeamish and tense that way, sometimes I behave impulsively. I blurted it out as the laughs quieted down.

"I was in Jack and Jill."

The ringleader of this particular piñata-whacking session fired back without missing a beat.

"Ugh, Chad . . ." She scowled at me. "That checks out. Of course."

I visibly winced but tried to play it off. Her response carved into my gut because I knew I was isolated, once again, from the others in the room. Now they were insiders and I was an outsider. Just like when Daron saw my parents' house. Just like when the kids at my middle school saw me in class with the white kids. Only this time I had outed myself. I was in violation of an important code of Blackness: We struggle *together*, no matter how much money you have or who vouches for your family. I had been a part of a group of people who formed an inner circle within that struggle that marginalized the others. I felt ashamed.

In the weeks that followed, I felt a few of my colleagues look at me differently. Or maybe I projected that, because I felt seen and vulnerable in a way that I had meant to hide from them. I'm not sure, partially because all of our interactions occurred via Zoom screens. I was one of only two writers based outside of Los Angeles, so I wasn't able to attend the small get-togethers and watch parties that they had during the course of the job. I was able to connect in person with Issa and our showrunner, Syreeta, and another of the writers, Kid Fury, in New York when we shot the episode I co-wrote, which took place in Brooklyn. But it was a week focused on shooting, not socializing. I wished I had more time to spend with the team, to show them who I *really* was. Or who I really wanted to be.

Our season was a success and the show was renewed for a season 2 on HBO Max. But as time went on, I started to hear buzz that the writers who would be returning to work on season 2 had already been selected. I reached out to one of my colleagues on the show to confirm, and indeed, I was not asked to return to the writers' room. My understanding is that budgets were tightened around the show, as they were all over the industry, and thus, the writers' room for season 2 would be smaller. I was proud of our work in season 1 and its cultural impact. And I got to fulfill a dream by working with Issa and the other writers, and I even got to appear in the episode I wrote. Still, I wonder about how that moment, when I outed myself as a Jack and Jill–er, affected my perception among my fellow writers.

What hurt the most was that I'd tried to hide the parts of myself that were formed in Jack and Jill and Black elitist culture so my colleagues wouldn't notice. I've tried to undo Black elitist doctrines in my mind and behaviors. I actively shun a way of thinking that says that some of us are better than others because we have more, speak a certain way, and are generally more palatable to white people. But once the smell is on you, it's hard to rub off.

And when I outed myself and the ringleader said "of course," she was letting me know that she had sniffed me out all along. Something gave me away. Maybe it was how effortlessly I code-switched. Maybe my slang felt forced. Maybe it was my posture, or my face, or my haircut. These were all elements I'd spent years getting just right so I'd never have to feel isolated from my own people like I did as a middle schooler. Yet even so, I'd been caught as an imposter, one of *those* types of Black folks, even before I announced myself as such.

The ringleader in the writers' room and my friend in Martha's Vineyard made clear the harm done by organizations like Jack and Jill and the general population of the Black elite, but they didn't need to. From the inside, I had my own point of view on the toxicities within those groups. Even as a kid I noticed that the relationships between people in those communities seemed profoundly manufactured and transactional. There was even a hierarchy within the geographical layout of the Jack and Jill organization in our region. The Washington, DC, chapter was the most posh, then ours in Montgomery County, then the Prince George's County chapter.

At events I saw a dry and forced tone in conversation between the adults. It felt like people were reading from a script. If two people were meeting for the first time, they'd tell each other where they went to college, where they lived, including noteworthy and esteemed street names, and what they did for a living within the first two minutes. If someone else were introducing those two people, they'd give up that information as part of the intro.

"This is Jon! He's a doctor, and he and Marla live on Sixteenth Street. He went to Harvard just like you, so you two *must* get to know each other." Then a handshake. Then a dry joke. And then guffaws.

The exchanges seemed to be missing the soul collision I felt when Black people met for the first time in other, less contrived environments like family reunions, cookouts, and AAU basketball games. I hate to say it, but the feeling in those Black elite rooms reminded me of the cold distrust I often feel in rooms full of white people. I'm usually in those rooms for business, transacting. I think the elders in the Black "elite" community learned that way of relating from corporate environments, Ivy League universities, and country clubs where white people dominate and their culture pervades. I think our elders brought the condescending, hierarchical way of relating from those spaces back into our environment like bees returning to a hive after being exposed to a slow-affecting, contagious insecticide. I see my peers—now the adults—doing the same.

As an adult I can see that I want to be free of this community—or for the community to change. Even as a child I could see that I was only partially a member. Yes, we were in Jack and Jill. But we were a suburban family with no Ivy League graduates, no fancy cars, no house on Martha's Vineyard. We didn't speak the language of posh society. We preferred basketball games and camping trips to country clubs and tucking our shirts in and talking about who got promoted. As a family, we sometimes had long debates about whether we'd attend events like balls and dinners thrown by *the elite*. We didn't want to spend the time and money putting together acceptable outfits to fit in with that crowd, and we knew that when we arrived we'd be sized up and condescended to. We were the charming, nice, suburban family. We were smart and educated, but we were not *fancy*. One foot in, one foot out. We wanted to feel included for the benefits, but we also felt pushed out by the culture of elitism.

But I can't deny I spent much of my life on the inside of that circle, which means that I've always had to overexert to endear myself to the people on the outside of this circle because that's who I want to love me most. Don't you see me doing that right now?

But that sort of overexertion is exhausting. And it's fruitless. After all, the stink is still on me.

16

The Cost of Living

I spent the first six years of my new career as an artist in financial panic because it was so hard to make money as a writer. It's not revelatory to say that it's difficult for creatives to sell our work, but even when I was able to sell my first TV series to BET and my first book to Simon & Schuster, there was the added complication of actually getting the money into my bank account. The process of finalizing deal terms, signing contracts, and eventually receiving that first deposit for my projects took months. As a newcomer, I didn't anticipate the long, stressful waiting period, and I was financially stretched and unnerved. In those periods I used to call my agent, manager, and lawyer every single day until the first check arrived, and when it did, it was only a small fraction of the entire deal, just enough to live on while I completed my creative obligations for the project. After commissions were paid out of my earnings to my representatives, I took what was left and used it to pay overdue bills and my very lean living costs at the time.

And I was one of the lucky ones. I was fortunate to be able to sell my projects at all and to have a legitimate team to negotiate reasonable compensation for my work. The entertainment and media industries capitalize on the cheap and free work of young, unrepresented talent like I was at the time; people who are so hungry and eager just to be accepted by the system and to have a chance for their work to be published that they'll take any opportunity, no matter how exploitative, to fulfill that dream. When I was in my late twenties and trying to get someone to buy my first TV series, I remember thinking that I would have done all the writing on the show for free just for a credit and an entry into the industry. As a matter of fact, I came pretty close to doing exactly that. I did quite a bit of free work for producers who promised me opportunities to work on their other projects (most of which never materialized), and I worked for free in exchange for places to stay when I visited LA and for invites to the right rooms. I wrote an entire sixty-minute drama TV series episode in two days for one particular producer, and I was never paid a cent for my work. That's sixty pages of screenplay. Before I joined the Writers Guild, I wrote a hundred-page screenplay for a very famous rapper and one of his marquee artists over the course of a week for an agreed-upon price of $4,000. I'm still waiting for my first dollar on that one.

I'm saying that I needed money and I needed opportunities and that the industries I work in prey on that sort of desperation just like every other industry in our capitalist society bloodsucks from the vulnerable.

As I write this book, we are entering the fifth month of the Writers Guild strike, in which our collective union of TV and film writers is in a cold war with our studio overlords over fair compensation for our creative labor as the threat of artificial intelligence looms.

Deadline ran a feature outlining the position of the studios who capitalize on our work. "The endgame is to allow things to drag on until union members start losing their apartments and losing their houses," a studio executive admitted.

This is a threat.

"I think we're in for a long strike, and they're going to let it bleed out," said another industry veteran familiar with the point of view of the studio CEOs.

This is another threat.

In so many words, the corporations are telling us, as creative contractors, that we must accept their conditions because they can outlast us in this cold war. Without income, some of us will lose our homes, some of us will lose our insurance, some of us will lose our access to prescription medicine and healthcare, some of us will "bleed out," some of us will die.

People are surprised by my visceral distaste for corporations and their overlords, especially as someone who started his career at Google when it was perennially named the world's greatest employer. That's like being named the world's greatest guillotine. Many of my old Google colleagues are being laid off daily to maximize profits for the company's top executives and its shareholders. These are people who started at Google right out of college and have given almost twenty years—their prime working years—to the company. These are people who have just recently signed mortgages on their first houses and who just started families. These are new moms and dads who traded the creative output and energy and brainpower of their twenties and thirties for the facade of protection by this giant, powerful company. And in exchange, when they needed stability most, they were given an ass to kiss.

And the same is happening for the creatives in Hollywood. The studios' position is that they'll "bleed us out," and that will be a literal reality for some of us. Given the economic demographic makeup of our country, I know a disproportionately large number of the most at-risk creatives in Hollywood will be Black and brown people. When people tell me that writers and editors and camera operators are driving rideshare around LA to pay the bills, I know that many of those people are Black, though there are few of us in the industry to begin with. As ESPN host Stephen A. Smith put it on his appearance on *The Bill Simmons Podcast*: "When white people catch a cold, Black people get pneumonia."

If the studios intend to squeeze the creatives into desperation, Black creatives will suffer first and suffer most. Today, I'm grateful that I'm somewhat protected, though not immune, from their suffocation. I'm a middle-class, Hollywood outsider. I never took the pill entirely, never moved to Los Angeles to forge my path in the Hollywood system. My distrust in establishments grew so strong in the tech industry that I could never let myself believe in the Hollywood ladder. As such, I had to find a few ways to support myself like writing books and producing podcasts. I've only ever written for two TV series: *Rap Sh!t* and *Grown-ish.* But if this strike took place just a few years ago when all my income came from selling my writing to Hollywood, I would have been devastated. And that's the position so many creatives find themselves in.

And to be clear, I'm still affected by this strike. I'm not rich. I'm in the middle class. I *need* the supplemental income that Hollywood offers me. I have no dependents and no mortgage, but my fiancée and I would like to buy a house and start a family in the next few years. That will be much more difficult if the studios replace writers like me with robots, as they intend to, and if their counterparts in the publishing and podcasting industries do the same.

This is the second major time I've faced the precarity of my career path without the mirage of corporate protection to help me sleep at night. Like many during the pandemic, I was under enormous stress watching my account dwindle as the studios all shut down production and not knowing if my transactions with them would stop entirely. But that was an act of God that everyone faced all over the world. I can accept that. This Hollywood cold war is the will of greedy studio executives, just little human beings, and yet they have such grave, life-and-death implications.

One of the thrills of my life is taking long walks with Penny Rihanna through our neighborhood in Queens. Even as an animal lover, I never imagined the love and attachment I'd develop for a big, slobbery German shepherd who doubles as companion and security guard.

When the weather is cool enough, Penny and I sometimes walk for more than an hour through Glendale, Forest Hills, and Ridgewood. I call these longer walks "thought marches." She gets to do her important work of smelling where other dogs have peed, and I get to do my work of thinking through a creative problem or a tricky paragraph in my head.

We once took a thought march through the snow so I could think through an advertisement I needed to produce for my digital content business. I loved the feeling of the two of us out there in New York's loud, aggressive chaos, with the cold air whipping in through the face opening in my coat. Those walks tap into something primal. I closed my eyes and imagined we were in the wilderness together, trudging through nature. That feels like freedom to me.

When I opened my eyes again, we were back on the corner of Onderdonk Avenue and Cornelia Street, standing in front of Rolo's, my favorite restaurant in the city. I go to the restaurant so often, they'll let

Penny come in with me briefly to order food to take out. On this day, I ordered a grape and olive focaccia and munched on it as we walked back out to resume our march.

We reached the end of the block and awareness thumped me.

I *thought* I noticed a grape missing from my focaccia. I looked down and saw scattered pieces of food from the restaurant on the ground. And Penny seemed to have something in her mouth. I grabbed her face and pulled her jaws open, shook her face a bit to see if something popped out. I'd successfully removed slobbery chicken bones and insects from her grasp in the past. But nothing appeared. Still, I had a feeling she'd swallowed a grape. Grapes can cause fatal kidney failure in dogs.

I rushed Penny twenty minutes on foot to the vet, all the while dreading that I had failed her as her caretaker. When we arrived, we sat in the waiting room for another twenty minutes of light dread. When the doctor and nurses showed, they were kind and gentle to Penny, but she was scared and so was I. They told me that the best thing they could do right now was to induce Penny to vomit so they could see if she'd ingested the grape.

The cost for the procedure: more than $500. I realize now thinking back on it that I would have agreed to pay any amount of money.

They took her in the back for an hour-long procedure. While I waited, I stared up at the wall at a framed photo of a German shepherd. More dread. I thought about my then fiancée and Penny and me. We called ourselves a pack. And I had failed the pack. I blocked my thoughts to avoid breaking down in that office; to avoid worrying that we'd had our last thought march together.

A woman from Queens came in and sat beside her partner a few chairs down from me. She was waiting to pick up her Goldendoodle, which had come for routine shots. She saw worry on my face. She was sure not to tell me everything would be okay, but she told me a funny story about her last dog, who would eat all the Italian food her family dropped on the floor during meals—olives, tomato sauce, noodles.

Finally, the doctor came out to the lobby. He was thin with brown curls. He was European, maybe Norwegian. He was gentle.

"Was it a red grape?" he asked.

I fumbled over my words, but was able to tell him that yes, it was.

They had induced vomiting with a shot four times, and Penny had puked it up. Relief surged through me, tempered by a pang of guilt—she'd gone through such an ordeal because I was lost in thought.

They brought my Penny back to me. I hugged her and stood to pay the woman at the front register. She rang up my receipt and read the price to me aloud. The procedure had in fact come out to roughly $500.

I heard the woman from Queens behind me gasp and whisper to her partner.

"That's crazy," she said. I think she said it loud enough for me to hear her on purpose. I think that was her way of showing sympathy.

But she knew what I knew. Penny is family. Everyone with a dog knows that. And I don't blame anyone without a dog for finding it ridiculous. But that's how it is.

I'm lucky. I had the $500, and even if I hadn't, I have friends who would've happily lent me $500 to save my dog.

But if that weren't the case, I still would have gone through with the procedure to save Penny. And then I would have figured out how to pay. I would have bent my morals around that decision if I had to. Maybe I would have stolen the money. Maybe I would have disappeared on the vet's office and the insurer. In this economy, maybe I would have had to break the law to keep our dog alive. Would I actually have the guts to do that? I don't know. But I think some would. I admire them. To me, that's having your priorities aligned.

Forty percent of Americans cannot come up with $400 in an emergency according to US Federal Reserve data. The average cost of an ambulance in New York is $1,400.

Now imagine that Penny was my daughter and not my dog. Imagine that I didn't have the money or insurance to cover the procedure. How much more horrified would I feel in that hospital lobby, waiting to find out if my distraction cost us a *real human family member*? The Money Lie would find me again in that lobby. Its haunting voice would come in and tell me that if I'd been a more diligent person, a more valuable American, with more money to show for it, that I'd be able to afford the procedure that would save our family.

When the studios say they intend to "bleed us out," this is what they mean. They mean they'll be all too happy to wait and watch the creatives who fuel their industry, the people whose work buys their mansions, their yachts, and *their* children's tuition, suffer real heartache and atrocity until we say uncle and accept whatever pathetic deal they offer. In our country, where for-profit healthcare and capitalism bear down on us in our most dire circumstances, money is a matter of life or death. It's quite literally the difference between saying goodbye to someone you love or having them in your life for another day.

I imagine all those millions of hospitalized people during the worst of the Covid-19 pandemic. I can see their family members' faces staring into nowhere trying to solve how they're going to pay to keep their loved ones alive. I imagine their horror facing the truth that their poverty could be a death sentence. I bet they blamed themselves for not having the money. I bet those who go into debt to keep people alive often come to resent those people later as new problems arise that need money for fixing and compound the misery in their lives.

And I can't ignore that the people who suffer most under capitalism are *still* the same people who were first capitalized on in this country in the slave trade: Black folks. Almost 20 percent of us live under the poverty line. That's more than twice the percentage of non-Hispanic white Americans.

We need money to survive in this country, and our corporate overlords are actively squeezing our necks to keep it away from us.

I used to try to be charming and likable when I worked with corporations. I would get to know the executives by name and chum it up with them when opportunities to do so presented themselves. I've felt the industry harden me. My exchanges with execs now are direct, if not curt, and my tone in emails is cold. I'm focused on the transaction, my work for their money. I try to set clear expectations that I'm here to provide a service and not a friendship. Sometimes I feel bad knowing that the executive I'm working with exists so many layers removed from the person at the top who is *actually* capitalizing on both me and the executive. But I'm not a saint, I'm a human, and the exec represents a group of people at the top who I know would "bleed me out" at a moment's notice.

So there's a new me, at least as far as business is concerned. Hardened. Frank.

This new way of being is directly related to the life-or-death value of money. It's stale but true to say that money cannot buy happiness. But money can buy medical procedures and insurance, and, if you're lucky, that means it might just buy you another day with someone you love.

That is the cruel truth we all live with in this country. And as long as the overlords have us trapped in their guillotine, bleeding us out each time we demand fairness, we'll never be free.

17

A Man Named Lunsford Lane

Lunsford Lane was born in 1803 to Edward and Clarissa Lane, enslaved house servants in Raleigh, North Carolina, working for Sherwood Haywood.

As a child, Lunsford sold a basket of peaches his father had given him. The experience sparked an interest in entrepreneurialism. He would later remark that at that time, "plans for money-making took the principal possession of my thoughts."

After Haywood died, his widow was forced to let Lunsford rent himself out for about $100–$120 per year. Lunsford saved some of this money to eventually buy his own freedom for $1,000.

Lunsford spent the rest of his life traveling between North Carolina, New York, and Boston, finding ways to make money, such as working as a tobacconist and delivering abolitionist lectures for pay. He used the money to travel back to North Carolina to buy freedom for his family members one by one. During his travels he was arrested multiple times—on false charges—and he was kidnapped by a mob and tarred and feathered in the woods.

Lunsford Lane learned how to make money as a child, became obsessed, made enough money to buy his own freedom, then spent his remaining years risking his life to do the same for his family. This is a profoundly common story, the story of obsessing over earning money to exchange for freedom, for Black people in the United States, even today. I'm driven to earn to keep the freedoms I have and to try to expand them for myself and my family. I wasn't born into slavery like Lunsford, but I think about it every day. Like Lunsford, plans for money-making have taken the principal possession of my thoughts. I've seen my friends arrested and imprisoned for crimes of poverty. I've seen them murdered for getting involved in petty crimes and drug sales because they needed money to feed themselves and their children. I was born several generations removed from slavery, and into a family able to offer enough comfort and stability that I wouldn't have to commit similar crimes. Yet I'm reminded constantly that America's prisons are filled with modern-day slaves who look just like me. And our streets are stained with the blood of Black people indicted on false charges and killed by mobs without trial. So I run from that fate, like Lunsford, chasing the only glimmer of protection that seems attainable: cash.

I know that sounds stupid. I know money can't protect me from anti-Blackness. But what else is there? I'm asking honestly. If I left this country with my then fiancée in search of a place where Black people are treated as humans, equally deserving of life and protection, I'd leave behind the rest of my family, my parents, my sister, my three precious nephews. What about my cousins? What about my friends? Like Lunsford, I'd spend the rest of my life trying to earn enough money to offer them protection and obsessing over their well-being. Maybe my body would be safe, but my thoughts, like Lunsford's, would remain possessed.

I want to be free. I want my family to be free. So I'll try to get there by earning.

I relate to an irony that Lunsford must have felt delivering his abolitionist lectures for pay: I see the market opportunity for me to write and talk and make art about Black struggle. I see how it can be lucrative. I've taken the money, as fast as I can, hand over fist. I want it. I want it. I've made money giving talks about race to corporations and colleges. I am learning that the more honest I am in doing so, the more cashable my voice becomes. But I am ever aware of the people who are offended by my presence, my message, my honesty. And I mean to avoid the tar and feathers, or worse, that eventually came for Lunsford.

That presents a complex equation for me and other Black people who make money in a way that challenges whiteness. The more honest we are, the more money we make. Up until we approach some unknowable, moving threshold. Once we cross that line, when our voices become too honest, too defiant, and too valuable in a way that upsets white supremacy, there are consequences. I guess?

This is a fear we're taught. We come to understand that we can push back on white supremacy so long as we're entertaining and not threatening to its absolute rule. We see what happens to those who push too far or too hard. I feel an impulse to double down on that caution. I feel like my elders would tell me to be careful here, and to remind others that we should never write so honestly that we make ourselves targets. But that's someone else's story. I can't write that. I'm supposed to be free when I write. That's my contract with myself. I must be free on the page even if I can't be free in my body. If I forfeit my freedom to think and write honestly because I'm afraid of the consequences, what freedom is left for me?

And what of those consequences? Since starting down this path as a writer, I've pushed myself to be more honest and bold, first with myself, and then in my work. Thus far, I have been surprised to find that the fears that once scared me into thinking I'd suffer for my honesty were hollow. I'm young and early in my journey, but I would be thrilled to see each of us Black people be just 1 percent bolder in our approach to challenging anti-Blackness. I'd be thrilled for each of us to test the waters, to push the envelope just a little harder and see if the consequences we fear are real.

Will we really lose our jobs?

Will we really be outcast by families and friends who think we are behaving irresponsibly?

Will we be imprisoned? Will we be killed?

I'm not sure, but I think fear of these consequences holds a firmer shackle on our necks than the consequences themselves. Every image I see of a Black person shot down by police, of white supremacists marching with tiki torches, of pro-Trump rioters with their feet kicked up in the Capitol works to intimidate me. Those images of small groups of white people brazenly asserting their dominance push me to make myself small and subservient to white people everywhere.

In line at the mall. On a phone call with my agent. In the drunken stands at a football game.

But what if I just said "fuck it" a little more loudly each day?

What if I chose to ignore those acts of intimidation that signal to Black people that there is only one kind of freedom and that is white freedom? I'm not suggesting that I do anything drastic, just that I try to live 1 percent less fearful of the consequences of being Black today and another 1 percent more tomorrow. Some might call that irrational and dangerous. Others would call that an incrementalist outlook, choosing crumbs of freedom instead of striving to take the whole pie.

I think it's both. But if it works to make me feel freer, I don't care what anyone calls it. I can only imagine how liberating it could be.

What strikes me most about Lunsford's story is his solitude. I imagine Lunsford pausing to rest on one of his trips from North Carolina to New York. He's sitting in the shade of a tree drinking free water from a stream. He is looking out at a lush green meadow and the border of the woods some fifty yards away. There are no people in sight, and the midday sun is shining down from a blue sky. He can hear a few birds chirping in the distance and the soft rush of a stream nearby.

In this moment, Lunsford is free, having purchased his own freedom. He has paperwork to prove it. He began his life as an enslaved person and masterminded a path to liberty. Now he has coins in his pocket, and he is lying against a tree in a gorgeous field of soft grass. This is a place for luxury.

And yet, I imagine Lunsford's mind is anywhere but in this paradise. He's trapped by the mission. He is thinking about where he'll go next, how he'll make the money he needs to buy freedom for the people he loves, one by one. He is thinking about the hell that awaits him if he missteps, and the hell that still engulfs his family. He is thinking about his safety and plotting to increase his narrow odds of making it back to his parents, his children. He is clutching his freedom papers, which will give him the slimmest chance of protecting himself legally the next time the slave-capturing police arrest him and take him to court.

Lunsford is "free" but not free. All around him is nature's beauty, and all that he can see is the urgency of the moment. How tragic and how common for Black people.

Can he even feel the warmth from the sun on his legs and cool from the shade covering his neck? Can he hear the babbling stream? Can he take deep breaths to breathe in the clean air from the woods and the grass around him?

Not in my snapshot. In my snapshot, his body is there in nature and his mind is in the gears of his mandate: money-making. Freedom. He is possessed.

I relate.

I have spent most of the last seven years making art while trying to make money. This was my mission of freedom. In a way it was selfish.

I could have struggled up through the corporate system striving to make millions of dollars. Maybe I could have invested that back into my family and our community. Instead I've straddled the line, torn by the mission to earn and the pursuit of creating purely. I feel so strongly inclined to chase money, but I want just as badly to live and to create freely. And that tension tears me in half. It eats at me.

But it doesn't hurt nearly as bad as living my days in a cubicle. Each day I spent in corporate America made me more angry and sad to live a life I didn't believe in for money. I felt myself starting to project that on the people I loved. I felt myself trying to bury it and ignore it, but that ruined my sleep. Over time I would have found ways to settle into my sadness, drinking it away at Martha's Vineyard country clubs and golf courses.

I'm blessed just to have money and employment, I'd tell myself. That would soothe me. And in fact I *was* lucky to have employment, and I was lucky again to find a path out of that employment through writing. And every day I sprint toward the next opportunity and the next dollar, urgently running away from having to shuffle back into the confining depression of that cubicle, if anyone would even hire me at this point.

I live a happy life. My family is healthy. I make enough to support myself. I live in a nice place in New York City. My brain and body are active and challenged and treated. I see beauty often. I talk to friends I love all the time. I feel free in many moments.

And yet, money-making can still possess my thoughts. Am I doing enough for *us*? Am I doing my part to help buy *our freedom*? Am I making enough to pursue my own freedom?

These are the thoughts that waft into my head when I'm lying in my hammock, in the backyard, listening to the rustle of the trees. Like Lunsford Lane.

18

Black People and Isolation

Freedom is so vital to me that it seems sacrilegious to define it. Unlike food and water, which we can survive several days without, the moment our freedom is taken, we die. When I'm not free, I don't exist anymore. I'm someone different entirely, someone who belongs to someone or something else. But that someone is not me, and it doesn't become me again until I have my freedom again. I'm not myself, but someone whose entire purpose is bound to the mission of trying to become free again, so that I can live.

Taking someone else's freedom is the ultimate crime. To take someone's freedom for even a moment is to kill them for a moment. Anyone who would take another person's freedom willingly is a monster. Anyone who would willfully ignore that they are taking someone else's freedom is an ignorant monster.

I'll try to define the vital force that is freedom. It's weightless. It makes my head and body lighter and my heart skip a beat. It looks like a green, open meadow surrounded by woods. It looks like deep space and the deep sea. It looks like clear, blue water with coral that you can see fifty feet down to the bottom.

But freedom doesn't need to be so abstract or so natural.

Sometimes I have freedom for a moment. When I'm not thinking about how my point of view will be judged. When I can forget for a second about the various missions and habits that propel me each day. Making money. Getting out from under white supremacy. Doing enough. Being enough.

The times when I feel most free are when I feel connected to everything and attached to nothing. I feel that way walking through Forest Park in October wearing a hoodie and cargo pants listening to "Love Is Stronger Than Pride" by Sade. I feel that way sitting in the backyard with a bonfire going while Penny Rihanna chews on a big piece of wood after her dinner. I feel that way leaving dinner in Bed-Stuy, driving across the Williamsburg Bridge to meet a friend for a drink at a speakeasy on the Lower East Side. I feel that way in the woods in Woodstock and swaying to "All the Way Turnt Up" by Roscoe Dash in a club full of Black folks in Atlanta.

I can name the places and moments where I feel connected because they are rare moments of bliss, pockets of air that fill me up to keep me going until I get to feel them again. America intentionally enforces isolation on Black people by design. I've felt the watchful eye of police, white neighbors, security guards, teachers, "friends," and coworkers since my early teenaged years. I've felt their gaze and heard their scared, aggressive tones instructing us to separate and move away from each other. When we were younger and thinner and bouncier in our twenties, our gentrifying white neighbors in Brooklyn would intentionally walk between us instead of around us on sidewalks to assert dominance and move us apart. Police pay me noticeably more attention on interstates when I'm driving with one or two Black friends in the car. When I worked at Google, I felt the judgment from my non-Black colleagues who walked by the "Black table" in the cafeteria where Black employees congregated to catch our breath from time to time. One colleague—a Black woman who passed when she chose to—warned me not to sit at that table too often or I'd be branded a non–culture fit. I took her advice and began avoiding the Black table.

But even as I did what she suggested and isolated myself, I thought to myself that she must be exaggerating. It seemed absurd that our white colleagues would be made uncomfortable or intimidated by us congregating. After all, they outnumbered us significantly just as they did in the rest of this country. I thought about how long I'd been aware of this unwritten rule, that we shouldn't congregate or else we'd make white people afraid and then they might try to hurt us. My dad told me and my friends when we were just learning how to drive as teenagers that we shouldn't have more than two of us in the car at once or we'd be putting ourselves in danger. I thought about teachers separating me and the one or two other Black kids in my mostly white classes on the seating chart all through grade school. But I always tried to shrug off the idea that Black isolation was intentional because it's unbearably sinister to make people feel alone on purpose. We *need* connection.

And then I went to visit the National Museum of African American History and Culture in Washington, DC, forty minutes from my hometown. I had been warned that the darkest and most moving floor of the museum was at the bottom of the slave ship, so that's where I ventured first. There I found a remarkable number of photos, sculptures, and illustrations depicting slavery and the middle passage in what I experienced as haunting honesty. There were spare explanatory cards beside each work in the quiet, dimly lit halls of the museum.

One passage stays with me.

> *It shall not be lawful for more than five male slaves, either with or without passes, to assemble together at any place off the proper plantation to which they belong.*
> —***ALABAMA SLAVE CODE 1833***

My hands shake as I write the words. The isolation I've felt so often and for so long as a Black person is not coincidence or imagination. Loneliness is not an emotional defect I was born with. "Minority status" for Black people is not a matter of population size.

All of this—isolation, loneliness, always feeling like "the only"—was, and therefore in many ways still is, the law. The law stated that groups of Black people were not to congregate away from places where they belonged to white people as property.

Why does it still feel this way?

I think today about places where Black people are encouraged by white people to congregate in groups of more than five.

Sports teams.

Prisons.

Record labels.

Places where white owners and executives capitalize on and govern Black life. Places where we are not free.

There are some other places where Black people congregate that seem frowned upon by white people. Take HBCUs for example. I've never felt more connected than when I was a student at Morehouse in Atlanta, Georgia. A Black kid at a Black school in a Black-ass city.

But soon after I graduated, I noticed white people looking at me as someone who was smart, with a high potential to succeed *despite* the fact that I'd come from a Black school. All that congregating in a place not owned by white people was a violation of that old Alabama ordinance. As a result, they would not value our degrees as highly as the Bowdoin and Yale and Stanford degrees our friends earned by serving their time in isolation at predominantly white institutions.

And the isolation scales up. I can't buy my way out of it. Billionaire businessman LeBron James was diminished by Phil Jackson, who himself failed miserably as a league executive, for hiring and working with Black friends as business partners.

When referencing LeBron's time playing for the Miami Heat, Phil Jackson said this to ESPN:

> *When LeBron was playing with the Heat, they went to Cleveland and he wanted to spend the night. They don't do overnights. Teams just don't. So now [coach Erik] Spoelstra has to text [Heat president Pat] Riley and say, "What do I do in this situation?" And Pat, who has iron-fist rules, answers, "You are on the plane, you are with this team." You can't hold up the whole team because you and your mom and your posse want to spend an extra night in Cleveland.*

Today, LeBron's team of Black friends, agents, and confidants are one of the most savvy and powerful business groups in pro sports. But what Phil saw violated the old code: too many Black people in one place working for what they wanted.

A version of LeBron with white agents, managers, accountants, handlers, etc., would be more palatable. There, surrounded on all sides, isolated, he could be more easily controlled. Monetized. Discarded.

19

Thoughts from a Therapist

In my corporate journey that started at Google, and now in my trek through Hollywood, I've felt the damaging effects of Black isolation, once mandated by slave codes, that remains in our country's cultural fabric. The signals that we must separate and move alone if we want to ascend are so subtle that it's hard to prove—to ourselves and others—that they're real. How can I explain to someone that my white colleagues at Google looked at me differently when I sat with other Black employees at lunch? How can I get someone to understand that Phil Jackson is dismissing LeBron and his Black business partners as some sort of juvenile gang if the person I'm trying to persuade would rather not see what's there?

Many deride the competition between Black people climbing in our careers, trying to get the big job and the big check. Personally, I feel the tension between my spirit, which wants to love and connect with other Black people in all environments, and my mind, which tells me that our opportunities are finite and that I have to be that one, special Negro to get that next greenlight, that bonus, that promotion. That competition between us seeds profound loneliness. When I read the Alabama Slave Code in the museum, I was heartbroken. As familiar as I am with the evils of this country and the way it treats Black people, that ordinance revealed something darker than slavery itself: White supremacy doesn't just want Black people to suffer, it wants us to suffer alone.

When I'm alone in the park in a white neighborhood, I'm more vulnerable to a predator. When I'm alone in a business meeting with executives and fast-talkers, I'm more vulnerable to take a bad deal. When I'm alone in a corporate office, I'm more vulnerable to be told I'm misinformed, undereducated, or crazy.

Jordan Peele portrayed the life-and-death stakes of Black isolation in his magnum opus, *Get Out*, in which a young Black man named Chris is preyed on, captured, and almost decapitated by his white girlfriend's family and their community because he's isolated from his people and susceptible to gaslighting. In Peele's film, the only two people who try to save Chris are both Black: first, another Black captive who yells at Chris to *GET OUT*, affirming Chris's suspicions that something dangerous is afoot. And finally, in the film's closing minutes, the protagonist is saved by his Black friend Rod, who drives all the way from the city to the suburbs to save him.

The message of the film is poignant: Isolated in whiteness we are at incredible risk. I felt the pain of that isolation even before I understood it in my early twenties working in a Silicon Valley cubicle. I felt that pain in the hotel lobby in Florida on "vacation." I felt it in Forest Park, alone with Gary as my tour guide. I felt that pain of isolation in the hotel lobby in Israel while Ira and a few others chortled at me and people like me as the butt of their joke. I feel it every time I walk into a place where Black people are made to feel unwelcome.

When I enter spaces among the white and privileged to try to seize opportunity, I'm so often isolated, with no one else like me to affirm my experience, which leaves me susceptible to gaslighting. Black people have experienced gaslighting—being made to question our sanity—for centuries. The conversation around Black people being gaslit in the workplace, where we go to earn, has gotten louder in recent years. I know that. I feel it in the moment. But so often I just shrug off the bad feelings to make it through the day, the week, the year.

But I can feel that these experiences damage me over time. So, I asked my friend Amanda Jurist, a licensed clinical social worker and family therapist, about the effects of isolation and gaslighting. We connected on a Zoom call where she walked me through some of the physical and psychological effects of these common experiences for Black people.

"Being in a setting where you're constantly gaslit creates a person that is extremely anxious. Highly depressed. Disconnected from their body," she said. "They might start to experience symptoms such as tingling in the hands and feet. You might experience shortness of breath. I get a lot of people describing this feeling of a knot in their chest. There's nothing technically, medically wrong with the individual, but because they're so emotionally bound because of the gaslighting, they've learned not to trust themselves. Because someone's constantly convincing you that what you're experiencing is actually not happening."

I thought about my experience in the woods with Gary and the guy in the hotel lobby who commented on my hair. In both instances my body was telling me I was in danger, but I was paralyzed. I thought about times I've been surrounded by whiteness in classrooms and offices, times when I was poked, belittled, and insulted by white people but unable to trust my feelings enough to defend myself. These were times when I'd look around the room to see if anyone else felt what I felt or recognized that I was under attack, and all I'd see were uninterested and unempathetic white faces. And so instead of defending myself, I froze, doubting my own feelings, and then later I doubted myself for being unable to protect myself in the moment.

Amanda continued to explain the physical damage that these experiences can have.

"So [the person] is emotionally bound in a way where there can be this tightness, this tension carried in the chest area. I've heard people, especially women, describe this feeling of gasping for air and feeling like they're having a heart attack, but it's really a panic attack. So they're still operating and doing their job in this state of panic and tension and angst. That's why they get used to living in that space. Operating outside of that becomes very, very foreign. It becomes typical to have a very anxious work experience and carry that very anxious experience into personal relationships with family and friends as well. So it causes tremendous pain."

So often Black women are called crazy. So often Black men are called angry. Maybe this is why we seem that way to people who don't understand our experiences. As I listened to Amanda, speaking in her gentle but clinical and deliberate voice, my body shifted around. I noticed the stiffness in my neck, back, and shoulders. I could feel the tension I was living with from more than thirty years of these harmful experiences that began in childhood.

But until this conversation I had never taken much time to examine the effects of all those moments of isolation and gaslighting. And until a few years ago I had never tried therapy, or anything else healthy, to deal with the long-term feelings of loneliness, stress, and anxiety I have suffered from years of enduring anti-Blackness and white supremacy. I was reluctant to try therapy because it's expensive and only 4 percent of mental health professionals are Black. I couldn't trust someone who isn't to help me deal with these difficult and complex feelings. There are many Black people who are similarly reluctant to try therapy. Only 9.8 percent of Black people in the US receive mental health treatment.

But Amanda tells me there are important reasons why Black people avoid therapy to deal with our internal and physical pain besides the steep costs of treatment and the lack of Black mental health professionals.

"When you think about Black, African American individuals, the experience of slavery, the results of what that did to our people and our communities are just endless. The pain, the dehumanization, the pattern of internalizing yourself as the oppressed. And also experiencing oppression, racism, Jim Crow, segregation, these structural systems that continue to put Black Americans at a disadvantage. It is actually unsafe for someone to sit down and ask a person who is going through that much trauma to bare their emotions. If we think about a woman or a man on a plantation, there was no way that there was room to ask them how they felt. Do we really want to know what they felt, and could the psyche actually hold what would come up? There's no space for it from a survival standpoint."

Now Amanda was revved up. Her tone grew more passionate, more grave than before.

"So you see that kind of evolve. We've moved ahead in some areas, but still we're just focused on how to put food on the table, how to keep a roof over our heads, how to fight to get our children educated. We do not ask how we feel. 'When a feeling comes up in this house, it better stay in this house, and we're not getting into it.' It's a survival tactic. And so fast forward to now, we're still there. We haven't outgrown that state.

"Some people are so embedded in their trauma that we have to be very careful about the therapy they're even able to engage in because opening them up too wide can actually be detrimental to them."

Amanda is telling me that processing the trauma from slavery and racism and anti-Blackness can be harmful to someone focused on trying to earn and survive and move forward. I'm that exact kind of person, the person focused on earning and forward movement. The person for whom processing race trauma can be dangerous. And I made processing race trauma for public consumption *my job* because I wanted the money so bad.

20

I Quit

I reflect often on my conversation with Amanda. Here's the part that runs through my mind over and over again:

> *When you think about Black, African American individuals, the experience of slavery, the results of what that did to our people and our communities are just endless. The pain, the dehumanization, the pattern of internalizing yourself as the oppressed.*

The last five words eat at me: "*. . . internalizing yourself as the oppressed.*"

In the last few years of my life, I've done just that. When George Floyd was murdered, the publishing market opened up for my voice as a writer frustrated with anti-Blackness in America. I jumped in with both feet. I wrote screenplays and op-eds and a book about feeling oppressed. I sold my pain to pay my bills. I took money from corporations to share my pain. I even gave several talks at Google, where

I had been so painfully marginalized as a young, Black employee right out of college. I leaned into becoming *the voice of Blackness* on podcasts opposite white co-hosts. I leveraged victimhood for money, clicks, and authority in conversations with white people.

I internalized myself as the oppressed.

I didn't just wear my victimhood outwardly. I didn't just sell my identity as *the oppressed.* I lived in it. I became paranoid, locking horns with white people in my neighborhood, at my gym, in my work life, seeing every conflict as a result of some sort of discrimination against me.

I made my world smaller. I pushed away white friends by ignoring them altogether or becoming so cold in our exchanges that they gave up on connecting. I became fearful of traveling to certain places like the beaches upstate, the Hamptons, the woods in Woodstock, because I embodied *the struggle.* A struggle that I didn't create; a struggle I'm not responsible for. I became so prickly and defensive that I accidentally even pushed my non-white friends away in the process.

I thought it would be worth it to live with my thoughts consumed by Black trauma if it meant I could create more purely, more potently from that headspace. I thought it would be profitable. But the thoughts are just too dark.

I spent more time thinking about prison in the last few years than ever before in my life. There are so many Black people incarcerated in America's unjust prison system. There are about 470K Black inmates in state or federal prison right now. There are only about 430K white inmates, despite outnumbering us by five times. One in six Black boys born in America can expect to be incarcerated in their lifetimes. Black people make up 13.6 percent of the population, but 53 percent of exonerations.

I think about those Black people in cages every day. I think about how many times I could have been one. I think about how I still can.

I think about all the family members who lose hours and days and years thinking about them, missing them, living "free" in the outside world but consumed by their loss.

My second cousin was recently sentenced to six to eight years in prison for an assault. I've thought about him every day since I found out a couple months ago. We don't have a relationship as adults, but we knew each other as kids. I can see his big, goofy smile and his loud, jolly laugh. He had a round face with smooth brown skin and two parents who loved him so much, their only child. He was a singer in a traveling boys' choir. I heard his bright, melodic voice. I can still feel his infectious, warm energy. And I think about all of that dulling, day after day, in a cage, like the hundreds of thousands of other Black people locked away—many for crimes they didn't commit.

And then, naturally, selfishly, I think about myself. Prison, not death, is my greatest fear. Freedom is vital, and to live under someone else's authority in confinement *is* death.

I reach for something, anything, that can save me, as a Black person, from wrongful imprisonment, America's most heinous crime. Obeying the laws isn't enough for us. The Money Lie tells me that being wealthy is the only thing that can protect me. I know it's a lie, but it's more palatable than the truth—that nothing can protect me.

So I've clung to that lie.

I've spent the last few years trying to get rich, selling the story of Black suffering in America. But every moment I spend obsessing about, writing about, and *embodying* my own oppression, I die a little bit. Every moment I spend reliving my traumas, imagining slavery, detailing Black pain, and excavating our horror stories to sell to media companies and publishers, I'm forfeiting the freedom that I *do* have. I may as well be in a cage in those moments.

When I escape those thoughts, I'm free. I have a partner who is brilliant and creative and beautiful and *alive*. I have a family that is loving and strong. I have friends who challenge me and see me and protect me. I have three nephews who are absolute, pure joy.

And I have a gift, writing. I can do so much more with it than retell the story of Black trauma in this country over and over in different ways. I thought I could use that gift to help our cause. Maybe I did, in some small way. But when I take stock of our circumstances as Black people, it seems that not much improves for us year over year. We remain incarcerated, in poverty, attacked and killed by police, undereducated and underfed at the highest rates of any people, just as we have since we were first brought to this country.

Progress often feels like a farce. In fact, given the recent increase of anti-Black and white supremacist movements poking their head aboveground since Donald Trump's term as president, there are strong arguments to be made that we're being pushed backward. While writing this book, a friend from college told me she cries in her car every month because of the racism of her boss at work in a Hollywood studio lot for a well-known TV series. A few days later, a mentor called to tell me that a white client on a Zoom call with twenty other white people joked that if he kept vacationing in the sun, he would end up looking like my friend who has dark brown skin. My friend said the rest of the room guffawed while he turned off his Zoom screen. Nobody noticed. And just a day later, a close friend from childhood, almost a brother to me, called in tears, distraught that he'd been laid off by *another* Denver tech startup because he wasn't a "culture fit."

I can't stand to watch us being bullied, so I'm tempted to keep trying to fight back with what I have, words on the page. Like many others, I've tried to use my voice to make my point of view known: If there are white people out there who *truly* want to help us, then give us reparations; prove your intentions with *money*. Make your payments on the unaccountable debt of slavery.

I've said it, I've written it. Many others have done the same. And our voices fall on deaf ears. It's a maddening cycle, and I can't spend the rest of my life in it. Many Black people have written more poignantly, spoken more boldly, and given more of themselves to fight for our humanity. They'll never stop. I love them and I'm grateful for them. They're stronger than me. I'm exhausted. I'm tired of thinking and writing and speaking about our struggle.

I lose too much sleep. I absorb too much pain. I carry too much anger. It costs too much, and it pays too little. That's a bad trade. One that I can't rationalize anymore, even in my most avoidant, delusional moments. Like Amanda said, I'm not emotionally equipped to think about slavery and its effects on us every single day.

I'm done *internalizing myself as the oppressed.* I don't want to sell pain for money anymore.

So this will be my last time writing about race.

For now.

Unless I need the money again.

Acknowledgments

Thank you to my agent, Eve Attermann, who I admire as a true professional. You have helped me carve the foundation for my career. You are a rare combination of honest and direct and kind.

Thank you to my editor, Ian Straus. I was protective of this book when we started working together and you handled the process with great thoughtfulness and curiosity.

I am thankful to everyone in my life who has given me compassion and support as I walk this uncertain path. That includes the friends who I talk to every day and those I haven't seen or heard from in years. Closeness is invaluable, but space can be underrated.

I am grateful for my family, who taught me the value of art early in my childhood. You kept our house full of books and surely you can see what an impact that made on me and Shannon. Thank you for letting me go to Sea World as a kid to get my first experiences on a TV set. I remember your applause at every piano recital, basketball game, and school play. Sometimes I think of those applause to get through moments of self-doubt.

Thank you, Shannon, for your steady enthusiasm. I'm lucky to have you as a tag-team partner in this industry.

I am thankful for everyone who has believed in me and demonstrated that belief with action. In alphabetical order: Amanda Cowper, Angie Martinez, Brené Brown, Chris Spencer, Cordae, Dax Shepard, Ed Bailey, Emily Graff, Issa Rae, Julie Bowen, Leon Chitman, Morgan

Freeman, Morgan Williams, Monica Padman, Oronde Garrett, Rachael Field, Rob Holysz, Rose Catherine Pinkney, Spike Lee, and Vanessa Spencer. I've left so many people off this list, but I am thankful to you too.

Thank you, Roxane Gay and Jia Tolentino. I don't know you, but your work inspires writers like me to be brave.

I'm thankful for the countless people who have offered me their ears, eyes, and hard-earned money by following my work. I am so blessed that I get to share my stories with you. I hope they remind you that you're not alone.

Thank you for buying this book.

About the Type

The body of this text is set in Minion Pro, which was designed by Robert Slimbach as an Adobe Original typeface. Though the original Minion font was released in 1990, Minion Pro, with its simple elegance and high legibility inspired by late Renaissance typefaces, was released in 2000. Its classic style, larger aperture, and range of optical sizes make it an ideal choice for text that transitions from body to headings to caption-size small print.

The screenplay is set in Courier, which was originally designed by Howard "Bud" Kettler in the mid-1950s for use on IBM typewriters. Kettler considered naming it "Messenger," but opted for "Courier" due to the "dignity, prestige, and stability" of the word. The font is distinctly monospace, meaning that all its characters fill the same amount of horizontal space. Courier has been renewed and adapted as a computer font since the 1990s and is widely used in digital computing. Fittingly, it's become an industry standard to write all screenplays in 12-point Courier.

About the Author

Chad Sanders is the author of *Black Magic: What Black Leaders Learned From Trauma and Triumph.* He is the host of the *Yearbook* podcast on the Armchair Expert network and the Audible Originals podcast *Direct Deposit.*

Chad's work has been featured in the *New York Times, Time, Fortune, Forbes,* and other publications. Chad has also written for TV series on HBO Max and ABC Freeform.

Chad was raised in Silver Spring, Maryland, and earned his bachelor of arts degree in English at Morehouse College. He lives in New York City.

Instagram: @chadsand

X: @chad_sand

HowToSellOut.co